UKRAINE:

EUROPE'S BEST-KEPT SECRET

An Insider's Guide

Maria Kachmar

First edition 2016   ISBN   978-1540405166

https://www.facebook.com/UkraineEuropesBestKeptSecret/
mariakachmar.books@gmail.com

Ukraine: Europe's Best-Kept Secret, An Insider's Guide.
In this three-part book, the author invites you to get to know modern-day Ukraine. She encourages you to visit Ukrainian cities, particularly Lviv and Kyiv, and other beautiful spots of historical importance or natural beauty. She also invites you to explore the Ukrainian culture, cuisine, belief system and more. This book is meant for tourists, virtual nomads in search of a new location, expats relocating to Ukraine, and all those interested in learning more about the Ukrainian way of life.

TABLE OF CONTENTS

ACKNOWLEDGEMENTS

This book is dedicated to my late father, Alexander Wsevolod Kachmar, born in 1940 in Lviv. If not for my father's determination to raise me as a Ukrainian-speaking patriot of our ancestral homeland, I would not have had the inclination to come to live in this fascinating and beautiful country. It was with him, and my mother, in 1998, that I first travelled to, and fell in love with, Ukraine.

I also owe much gratitude to my husband Steve, who supported me in many ways with this project. His shared enthusiasm enhanced our family's experiences during our Ukrainian adventures.

I would also like to thank all of the wonderful Ukrainians who enriched our time spent in Kyiv and Lviv. I share the hopes and dreams of millions of Ukrainians that this country will one day reach its full potential and blossom under a just government working for the people, allowing many to be freed from a life of struggle and injustice. I believe that tourism, which can contribute to the nation's economy and increase shared experiences between Ukrainians and non-Ukrainians, is one of way of helping to achieve this goal.

FOREWORD

As slumbering giants of tourism go, they probably don't come much larger than Ukraine. Overlooked by the geopolitics of its past within the former Soviet Union for most of the last century, Ukraine has been unsurprisingly by-passed by the travel imaginations of all but a few western visitors until recently.

Many foreigners, such as the author and myself, who have lived in post-independence Ukraine have enjoyed and become more enlightened by our experience and developed a strong affinity to the country. This helpful visitor and living guide invites you to do the same.

It is very important for any visitor to understand Ukraine's position as an emerging, dynamic country on the edge of Europe, one that embraces both the proud and unique traditions stretching back to medieval Kyivan Rus times and the ambitions and aspirations of European modernity. It is a country of contrasts and pleasant surprises that surpass the expectations of the shadowy understandings and stereotypes popularly held of Ukraine and its people.

Those who are looking to explore a 'road less travelled' are welcomed as guests to this undiscovered gem of a country and will experience the unique rewards of Ukraine's immense and unique beauty. No guide can truly convey the sense of grandeur, charm and love of life that Ukraine evokes, but this new addition will provide a set of invaluable reference points for the discerning traveller. Maria Kachmar's practical perspectives set the scene for great opportunities to explore the very best that Ukraine has to offer.

Good luck on your future Ukrainian adventures!

Steve Calland-Scoble,
Former Director, Pechersk School International, Kyiv

PART I – EXPERIENCE UKRAINE

INTRODUCTION

What does a visit to Ukraine have to offer? More and more people have been discovering the many attractions of Ukraine and seeing that day-to-day life is much less dramatic and much more pleasant than what is portrayed in the media. The two most popular cities, Kyiv and Lviv, have long been welcoming to foreigners. The capital, Kyiv, has had a growing expatriate population of diplomats and business people since Ukraine became independent in 1991. Lviv has experienced a small tourist boom as 'the next Prague' of Eastern Europe since its city centre was given a major facelift several years ago.

If you are interested in travelling to Ukraine to discover this hidden gem for yourself, then this e-book will give you an idea of what to expect once you are there in order to make your stay more enjoyable and hassle free. It should also save you time by providing options on what to see and do along with links to relevant websites, and offer insights into the culture. Despite the many tourist-friendly venues, this industry is still developing, and the amount of English language resources available for visitors to Ukraine is still relatively small.

This book is mainly for:

- **tourists** who would like to have a unique travel experience and are keen to prepare for their visit
- **freelance professionals** or **virtual nomads** who are looking for a great place to work remotely for a few months

- **students** who are planning to study at a Ukrainian university
- **expats** who are relocating to Ukraine with their company

What follows is a brief three-part guide. **Part I** of this e-book provides suggestions on many of the amazing experiences, services and products you can enjoy in Ukraine. **Part II** offers recommendations on restaurants, theatres, museums and other tourist venues to try. **Part III** gets into some practical details of staying in Ukraine, such as using local transportation and locating good health care facilities.

I was born in Canada to a Ukrainian-Canadian father and a Canadian mother. I grew up with the Ukrainian culture and have spoken Ukrainian my whole life. Despite that, I was hit with many cultural shocks when I visited Ukraine for the first time at the age of 18, particularly those related to its Soviet past. I have travelled to Ukraine many times and crossed the border in every conceivable way (by plane, train, bus, taxi, hitchhiking, and even on foot). I have lived in Ukraine with and without children; in Kyiv for eight years and in Lviv for two years at different times. Being bicultural and bilingual, I feel I have the advantage of both understanding the Ukrainian way of life at a deep level, and possessing the perspective to be able to relate this experience to others.

I have yet to meet someone who was not enchanted by Lviv's charms upon visiting it for the first time or someone who wasn't impressed by the grandeur and glamour of Kyiv. The architecture, the food, and the many tourist and cultural attractions of these cities all delight the senses. There is so much to learn about and discover in Ukraine.

I encourage you to make plans for a trip in the near future. At the time of writing (March 2016), you can still experience the authenticity and uniqueness of this fascinating country, before it is discovered by mass tourism and loses some of the uniqueness that can go hand in hand with integrating into pan-European culture (considering Ukraine's EU aspirations). While strolling around the centre of Lviv, it can be quite refreshing to discover that, though Lviv's Market Square has a similar design to other European old town central squares, it consists of many original Ukrainian eateries, cafés, galleries, museums and clothing design boutiques, and you will not find chains such as Zara, H&M, or Starbucks.

If you only have time for a short visit, I would recommend staying for at least 2 weeks; but to get a full Ukrainian cultural experience you would need to spend at least a couple of months there. Nationals of many countries can stay for up to 3 months per 180-day period without a visa; if you wish to stay longer, see the visa section at the end of the book. For me, the key to making a long-term stay in Ukraine as comfortable and enjoyable as possible, is, like in any country, finding your comfort zone. Part III of this book should be useful in helping with this.

Another reason to avoid delay in making travel

reservations is that the present situation with the currency allows for foreign money to go a long way in Ukraine, particularly outside Kyiv. For freelance professionals, the relatively low cost of rent, groceries, eating out and transport can make Ukraine an attractive and convenient place to relocate for the duration of an independent work project.

But consider the advice that you be sensitive to the locals and not flaunt your purchasing power; the currency crisis has resulted in inflation skyrocketing, driving living costs up for those earning a salary in the local currency. At present, in Lviv you can enjoy a specialty coffee in a trendy city centre café for about 1 USD, a tasty craft beer for the same price, or a full course meal for two in a restaurant for between $7 and $20. Taxi rides within the city generally cost about $1.50; tickets to an opera in either city range from $1-12. By spending your money in Ukraine, you are supporting the economy and local businesses.

I don't believe that you can travel to Ukraine and not be touched by the spirit of the Ukrainian people. Formed over centuries of oppression and struggle, not to mention the two 20th century forced famine-genocides, it is alive as ever due to the inner strength of its people, their deep love for the nation, and two recent revolutions. To foreigners, Ukrainians can sometimes appear severe or gruff on the outside, but underneath you will find they are kind, helpful and take great pleasure in spending time together, often over coffee or a meal. Thus, no text about Ukraine is complete without paying due respect to its citizens. I encourage you to enhance your sojourn by getting to know Ukrainians and the Ukrainian way of life.

You may be surprised to discover how much of a high quality experience you can have at most of the newer venues and how high the local standards can be when it comes to going out.

Nowadays, when Ukrainian entrepreneurs open a new eatery, tourist attraction or other enterprise, they usually know how to "do it right", with most striving to provide aesthetically pleasing and quality interiors, and in the case of restaurants, high quality ingredients and exquisite dishes. When entertaining guests for business or pleasure, Ukrainian hosts strive to make their visitors feel well taken care of.

The current war/frozen conflict in the East of the country is naturally a major concern for Ukrainians, who all follow current events to a greater or lesser extent, hoping and praying for peace. The situation hits home most with the families or friends of men who have been drafted, and there are often fundraising campaigns for families who have lost fathers or soldiers needing life saving medical treatment. Outside the conflict ridden areas (a small area in the East), though, the country is safe, and people go through their daily lives much as before, for the most part trying to make ends meet while still having time to socialise and celebrate one of the numerous Ukrainian holidays throughout the year.

Despite the wonderful things you may encounter in

Ukraine, there is of course a reason that Ukraine is not yet part of the European Union. Public services are lacking, cities aren't as clean as in Western Europe, and infrastructure isn't as well organized. Your first impression may be that of many others who visit for the first time – that Ukraine is a country of stark contrasts. As a tourist, however, you probably won't have to deal with or even see some of the more unpleasant realities of Ukrainian life that the locals endure, such as corruption and poor medical facilities.

If you stray away from city centres you will see a different reality, with buildings and roads sorely in need of renovations, and more signs of poverty. If you would like to experience that or take on some much-appreciated volunteer work, you won't have to look far. If you're interested in getting a glimpse of some of the harsher realities of day-to-day life in industrial Dnipropetrovsk in 2001, the book *Love and Vodka* by R.J. Fox provides humorous accounts of some of his sobering Ukrainian experiences.

Many people notice the unique vibe and liveliness that can be felt on Ukrainian streets, in cafés, and at places of work. If you dare to embrace Ukraine, you will find it's energy addictive and entrancing; it is a place where you can experience deep human connections and be inspired by beautiful art and other expressions of Ukrainian creativity that you will notice all around you.

Many also note Ukraine's enormous potential to flourish, based on its wealth of natural resources, and its hardworking, creative and intelligent people. The main obstacles remain beating corruption, reforming its judiciary and legal systems, and then shaping up its infrastructure. A shift westward towards Europe should be the country's ultimate goal.

In order to have a successful journey, you will need to be open-minded in terms of your expectations of services and prudent in your behaviour as in other places outside Western Europe and North America.

Here are some **initial basic tips** to having a successful and safe stay:

- **Keep tabs on your wallet** and phone at all times. An unguarded valuable item is an easy target for theft.

- **Carry a photocopy of your passport** with you in case of an accident or random check by police, particularly on the streets at night (this is a common warning, though I have never been checked).

- For a short stay lasting a few weeks, I would advise **bringing some foreign currency**, which can be easily and safely exchanged at numerous currency counters. When withdrawing cash from bank machines, only use machines located in banks or some five star hotels.

- **Always inquire about or agree on a price beforehand**, whether it be a taxi fare, a hair cut, or babysitting services.

- **Learn some basic Ukrainian.** You can get by with English, but many people don't speak English, and you won't be able to get a full Ukrainian experience without being able to communicate with the locals.

- Be aware that **Ukrainians generally start and end their day "late"** compared to Western standards. Schools often start at 9am, and work can start anytime between 8 and 10am, ending around 6, 7 or 8pm. Most shops and even some cafés don't open until 10am, and many close at 8 or 10pm. A small number of venues close for an hour lunch break, usually around 1pm.

Please keep in mind that the information included in this book is anecdotal, based on my personal experiences and my observations while in Ukraine. I have been very fortunate to have met and made friends with many highly educated and talented individuals in Ukraine, including journalists, musicians, writers, doctors, lawyers, actors, politicians, volunteers and community activists. Had I spent my time in a rural or industrial area in Eastern Ukraine, my observations would likely be different than those provided.

Note on currency: I have provided some examples of costs of products and services in Ukraine, usually listing a rough price in Ukrainian Hryvnias (UAH) and a rough equivalent in American dollars (USD). These prices reflect the costs at the time of printing.

Note on language: Accurate Ukrainian transliterations are used in this book such as Chornobyl, Odesa, Kyiv, and chornozem, rather than the Russian transliterations of Chernobyl, Odessa, Kiev, and chernozem which may be more familiar to the reader due to their widespread usage in Soviet times.

UKRAINIAN CITIES

Ukraine is the **second largest country in Europe** after Russia and before France. The capital city, Kyiv, is a booming, bustling metropolis with an official population of over 3 million, making it one of the most populous cities in Europe. It has a much more diverse national and cultural make-up than any other Ukrainian city. The 4 largest cities after Kyiv (Donetsk, Dnipropetrovsk, Kharkiv and Odesa) all have populations of around one million, and the next 4 largest have between 500,000 and 800,000. Other popular cities for tourists are colourful Chernivtsi, sunny Odesa, and cozy Ivano-Frankivsk, which is often used as a base for getting to the beautiful Carpathian Mountains in winter or summer. Kyiv and Lviv are considered the most "Western" cities in the country.

OTHER DESTINATIONS WORTH VISITING

Ukraine has many beautiful natural sites and landmarks of historical significance. Below are a few of the top sites worth making a trip to.

Kamianets Podilskyi This beautiful medieval town located in Khmelytskyi oblast offers a window to the past as you stroll along its winding roads and visit its traditional town square and grand castle.

Zbarazh Castle This impressive fortress is located near the city of Ternopil. Once you cross the drawbridge you can take a tour of the palace and learn about the rich history of this unique spot.

Sofiyivskyi Park Renowned in Ukraine for its beautiful design and variety of flora, this park was built by Polish Count Stanislaw Potocki and presented as a gift to his Greek wife in 1802. It is located in the city of Uman in the Cherkasy region.

Oleshky Sands / Oleshky Desert A little known fact is that Ukraine has the largest semi-desert in Europe, along the coast of the Black Sea, occupying a space of 161.2 km^2. Tourism to this unique destination has not been well developed, but you may arrange a guide (this is advised) and are free to camp overnight under the stars.

Daffodil Valley Many Ukrainians and foreign tourists travel here each spring to see the blossoming of the magnificent Daffodil/Narcissus Valley. Located near the town of Khust in Transcarpathia, this is a great side trip if you plan to visit the Carpathian Mountains.

Stone Graves For those interested in archeology, you might be interested in visiting Ukraine's Stone Graves. Some dating back to the Bronze Age and others to the late Stone Age are located in Zaporizhzhya Oblast near the village of Melitopol and by the village Nazarivka in Donetsk oblast. At the site near Melitopol there are also 65 caves with engravings from time periods spanning the late Stone Age to the Middle Ages.

LVIV, LWOW or LEMBERG

Lviv Market Square

No matter how many times we visit Lviv, the first few days of each trip are spent marvelling at the city's amazing culinary and cultural scene and abundance of unique attractions for tourists. Our first stops usually include indulging in Lviv's century-old coffee tradition at one of our favourite coffee houses, and tucking into a traditional Ukrainian meal at one of the numerous spectacular restaurants. And no visit is complete without attending an opera, play or ballet in one of the many theatres. In the summer months, we love to just take in the warm vibes, enjoy the street music, admire the local architecture and get a glimpse of the latest Ukrainian fashion trends, never ceasing to be impressed by the locals women's skill at gracefully manoeuvring the cobblestone streets in stiletto heels.

Lviv has many tourists exploring it's 14-17th century Renaissance style architecture and quaint, narrow streets year round, but at the moment, from the languages heard, one can gather that they are mostly from other Ukrainian cities, Poland, Germany, and a small amount from North America (mainly in the summer). On summer days and weekends throughout the year, Lviv's city centre can often be heaving with people keen to explore the many interesting and often hidden tourist spots found throughout. This city's proper Ukrainian name is Lviv, but it is known as Lwow in Polish, Lemberg in German, Lvov in Russian, and Leopolis in Latin. The city was founded in 1240 by Ukraine's only crowned Kyivan Rus era prince, King Danylo Halytskyi, who named the city after his son Lev.

The whole historic centre of Lviv is a UNESCO World Heritage Site. In fact, Lviv's *Ploshcha Rynok* (Market Square) often feels like an open-air museum of 19th century life. Walking around the square and surrounding pedestrian zone streets, you will find a multitude of appealing cafés, restaurants, and street vendors, as well as small museums, galleries, exhibits, and gift shops. You will also see Lviv's signature red and yellow trams, many still from Communist days, traversing the square every few minutes. In the winter there are markets and kiosks with mulled wine, and a skating rink set up right next to the city hall. Street musicians can be heard on almost every street around the Square, ranging from those playing enchanting melodies on the violin to others blasting out modern Ukrainian pop on their guitars. You might also run into characters such as Darth Vader, the Minions, or Minnie Mouse, who make their living by posing for photos with tourists.

Several Lviv restaurants brew their own beer and others offer food that was popular in Lviv in the 19th century or earlier. Historically, Lviv was multi-ethnic, and some of the street names, churches, and restaurants reflect their previous Jewish, Armenian, or Polish identity. Polish writing has been restored on some buildings from pre-World War II times.

As mentioned, Lviv is often considered by tourists to be a smaller version of Prague, and others compare it to Krakow. The first time my husband and I visited Lviv together, he made me laugh by jokingly exclaiming, "It's like the Ukrainian-speaking part of Austro-Hungary!"

I have always found that interactions with people in Lviv seem more polite than those in Kyiv. Historically, Lviv was under Polish rule for a lengthy time and was also part of the Austro-Hungarian Empire. Manners are similar to those in Poland, with the phrases "*Proshu pana / Proshu pani*" (Please Sir/ Please Madame) or "*Pereproshuyu*" (a form of "Excuse me" similar to Polish) being used in Lviv, but never in Kyiv.

If you're looking for modernity, you can find that in Lviv as well. A few large Western style shopping malls have opened in recent years, one with a skating rink and bowling alley. A newly renovated water park opened its doors in 2008. Most cafés and accommodation offer free wi-fi access.

With the abundance of activities available, and the approachability of the young generation, it seems impossible to ever feel bored in Lviv.

Lviv has a humid continental climate. Summers are generally very warm or hot, winters can be cold but without much snow, and rain is common in the spring and fall.

Lviv's 2013 official population was around 730,000, and that figure has now increased mainly due to an influx of refugees from war-torn areas and Crimea. Compare that to famous Salzburg, which has a population of around 150,000 and Prague, which has about 1.2 million inhabitants.

Skip to the **LVIV** section now if you'd like to find out about more specific attractions in Lviv including galleries, restaurants and activities for children. Also take note that the Lviv Tourist Office can be found right off Market Square on #29, Ploshcha Rynok, and online at the following site: http://lviv-tourist.info/en/

KYIV

Central Kyiv

While Lviv can be considered a haven for tourists, Kyiv is usually the Ukrainian city of choice for long-term expats. Most large companies, foreign embassies and international organisations have their headquarters in Kyiv. Compared to Lviv, it feels more like a modern Western European city (particularly the city centre), and you can find many of the same chain stores and eateries that you would see in other popular European destinations. With its official population of almost 3 million, consisting of Ukrainians from all over the country and a large expat community, it is easy to feel comfortable and blend in.

Because most of the country's wealth is concentrated in the capital city, it is home to Ukraine's most exclusive boutiques and restaurants, and is the city of choice for fashion designers, pop stars, up-and-coming artists and political experts. For successful Ukrainian professionals and the wealthy nouveau riche business and political elite, the quality of life in Kyiv can be very high; the middle and upper classes own renovated apartments, expensive cars, designer clothing and they employ nannies, cooks, and house keepers. They also vacation in Europe and other tourist spots around the world.

Compared to other Ukrainian cities, the work pace and standards in Kyiv are much more in line with what you might find in Western Europe. If you are interested in looking for work in Ukraine, you can check the local English language publications for openings in your field of expertise. Some of the jobs even offer salaries equivalent to what you might be earning in the West.

Kyiv also has a vast array of attractions for tourists. Though not as walking friendly or as easy to explore as Lviv, the extensive underground metro system is very efficient and can take you to most popular spots, and the taxis are relatively inexpensive.

Among the tourist attractions are the many golden-domed churches, such as the UNESCO status *Lavra* complex, the *Zoloti Vorota* replica ancient city gates, and the arts market on *Andriivskyi uzviz*. Kyiv is a perfect destination for those looking for a cultural holiday with theatre visits. Using this guide to determine which venues you are most interested in, you can plan ahead by checking out the upcoming performances on the websites and in some cases even buy tickets online in advance.

In Kyiv you can see a variety of architectural styles ranging from the 11th century to present day. There has been much development since Independence was gained in 1991, and the UEFA Euro 2012 football championship also provided the funding for new infrastructure; thus, you will see a fair share of modern buildings. Unfortunately, many were approved through bribery rather than based on their fit with the surrounding structures, which has resulted in some unsightly spots. But even these mishap buildings can't ruin the positive energy of this city, which many consider much friendlier, down to earth, and less congested than Moscow.

Despite my fondness for Kyiv, my first impression was that the people, particularly in the service industry, seemed less polite, and the way Ukrainian and Russian are spoken in Kyiv sounded more harsh to me than the gentle Galician dialect I was used to. But after 8 years of living in the capital city, I have to admit that I also absorbed a certain amount of assertiveness and New York style straight-faced aloofness with strangers. It often felt like the pace of life was too fast to afford time for pleasantries with unfamiliar individuals.

I love standing on Maidan Square, the very centre of Ukraine's capital, and the location of two revolutions within the last 12 years, and gazing at the grandeur of the imposing Soviet-era buildings lined up and down the main boulevard, the Khreshchatyk. I have very fond memories of weekends spent ambling down the 1.2 km long Khreshchatyk and onwards toward the

Dnipro river and perhaps down to Podil, the old quarter. Strolling down the wide and very long city centre streets is quite a common weekend activity for capital city inhabitants, along with shopping, meeting friends in restaurants or cafés, or enjoying the capital's arts or music scene. There are also nice attractive neighbourhoods in many areas of the city, as well as Soviet-era "dormitory" neighbourhoods, designed for those who only return home after work to sleep.

If you're looking for glamour and fashion, Kyiv is the place to visit. In order to admire Ukrainian fashion, go no further than a walk down your street. Ukrainian women seem to put much more effort, glamour and coordination into their outfits than fashionable Parisian women. Many men are also quite trendy. You can also attend the Ukrainian Fashion Week, which is held twice a year, or people watch at nice restaurants or clubs.

Most Kyivites adore their city and in moments of city pride will sing the chorus of the popular 1962 unofficial Kyiv hymn "How can one not love you, my Kyiv?" (*Yak tebe ne lyubyty, Kyeve miy?*). Due to the mix of people in Kyiv who facilitate an atmosphere of inclusivity, and the number of years I lived there, I too, feel justified at proud of classifying myself to a certain extent as a Kyivite.

Though Russian was widely spoken in Kyiv due to centuries of Ukrainian language bans and a policy of Russification in Soviet times, Ukrainian is now increasingly used. The language of instruction in schools is Ukrainian, and the vast majority of cultural and political elite are proud to speak their native language.

Like Lviv, the climate in Kyiv is humid continental, but with hotter summers and more snow in the winter months.

Please take note that Kyiv tourist offices can be found on #19 Khreshchatyk Street, #9 Pushkinska Street, or #7 Volodymyrska St. and more tourist information can be found on the following site: *http://www.visitkievukraine.com/*

For tourist information offices in **other Ukrainian cities**, please visit the following website: *http://www.touristinfo.lviv.ua/en/about/TIC_Ukraine/*

MANAGING WITH THE LANGUAGE BARRIER

Most street signs and other signage in Ukraine are in the Cyrillic alphabet. In Kyiv and Lviv, many street signs have been made bilingual in recent years and the Kyiv metro system now has an English voice over; nonetheless, having some knowledge of Cyrillic will still be an asset.

In our two main cities, it isn't difficult to find people who speak English to help you around. However, many non-Ukrainians do find it helpful to use a bilingual guide or have a local friend help them. If you would like to have the support of an English guide or translator, you can find them at the following site: *http://go2ua.com.ua/menus/view/lviv*

Also check the Lviv and Kyiv sections below for links to local tour guides. You may want to shop around in order to find a translator who offers the best price. It is often possible to arrange an interpreter with a car.

Lviv has many tour guides who speak English, German, Polish, French or other languages. Some tourist spots also offer information in those languages. The employees at the tourist information centres speak English, so they are a good resource to turn to with specific queries.

The best way to overcome the language barrier is to learn any words or phrases you may need for daily communication. If you'd like to learn the language in advance of your stay, here are two helpful websites for learning the basics.

http://www.ukrainianlanguage.org.uk/read/

https://www.duolingo.com/course/uk/en/Learn-Ukrainian-Online

Duolingo offers a free interactive language learning app for ipads or other tablets. Using the app to pick up some new Ukrainian words can be an entertaining way to pass your time while en route.

You can also find a Ukrainian language tutor at a reasonable price. One agency to try in Lviv is the Natalia Dyachuk agency and in Kyiv, Echo Eastern Europe. *http://www.runa.org.ua/ua/*   *http://echoee.com/*

The Facebook page Ukrainian Language and Culture School also offers Ukrainian lessons over Skype. *https://www.facebook.com/learnukrainian/*

The attraction and charm of learning the Ukrainian language is well summed up on the Duolingo site.

"Learn Ukrainian, the Eastern Slavic language considered as melodic as Italian and French. This intriguing language has persisted despite several periods of bans, generating prominent authors and beautiful folklore songs. Learn to converse with the warm-hearted people of Ukraine while discovering the country's beautiful land and colorful traditions."

Here is a list of basic survival words and phrases to get you by in Ukraine during your first few days.

Basic phrases

English	Ukrainian	Pronunciation using phonetic alphabet	Pronunciation based on the English alphabet
Good day! (Hello)	Добрий день!	Dobryi den	Dobray den
Hi!	Привіт! (use with friends)	Pryvit	Priveet
Good-bye!	До побачення!	Do pobachennya	Do pobachen-ya
Excuse me (Sorry)!	Вибачте!	Vybachte	Vibach-te
Please	Будь ласка	Bud' laska	Bood laska
Please (/You're welcome)	Прошу	Proshu	Proshoo
Thank you!	Дякую!	Dyakuyu	Dyakooyou
I need	Мені треба	Meni treba	Menee treba
How much does _cost?	Скільки коштує _?	Skilky koshtuye _?	Skeelke koshtooye?
Where can I find ___?	Де знаходиться?	De znakhodytsya	De znahodyt-sya?

Please pass me the ___.	Дайте будь ласка__. ***	Dayte bud laska__.	Daite bood laska. (ai as in 'eye')
Where is the WC / toilet?	Де туалет?	De tualet	De too-alet
Have a safe (and happy) journey!	Щасливої дороги!	Shchaslyvoyi dorohy	Shchaslivoyee dorohy

*** Please give me / Please pass me. This term is used very often in Ukraine and is very polite despite it being an imperative. It is used often in shops when you need to request an item behind the counter.

In Ukraine, strangers or acquaintances over the age of about 18 years old address each other with a level of formality and use the respective form "Ви" (Vy) (similar to *Vous* in French or *Sie* in German). They would never say something like, "Hi, how's it going?" to an acquaintance, sticking instead to a more reserved "How are your affairs?".

EXPERIENCE THE ARTS AND CULTURE

When in Ukraine, you will surely notice just how much the arts and culture are appreciated and enjoyed. Beautiful modern art, creative stage performances with intricately stitched costumes, hand-made souvenirs and even innovative interior design in cafés or shops are some expressions of the Ukrainian creative spirit.

There are so many aspects of Ukrainian arts and culture to enjoy, ranging from traditional theatres, operas, ballets, art exhibits, international fashion shows, classical concerts and more, to more contemporary creative work, such as elaborate street art, Ukrainian hip hop, experimental theatre, folk rock, folk punk, and Eurovision style pop music.

Both Lviv and Kyiv have many venues with different types of shows to attend. Arts options in Lviv are rich in creativity and national talent, easy to get to on foot, easy to reserve tickets, and incredibly affordable, while Kyiv events are sometimes on a more international scale with the large theatres having more of a feeling of grandeur.

Even without looking for it, you are sure to see some examples of the national folk arts, such as the rich, symbolic Ukrainian embroidery, weaving, pottery or other craftwork, and you may get a chance to hear one of the hundreds of beautiful Ukrainian folk songs, many of which date back centuries.

Ukraine has many interesting up-and-coming bands and artists. Three notable groups include the modern "ethno chaos" band **Dakha Brakha** with its ancient drum beats, the **Telnyuk Sisters**, a vocal duo who combine jazz, rock, blues and ethnic motifs, and **Okean Elzy,** one of Ukrainian's most popular rock bands. You can check out their videos on youtube to get a taste for modern Ukrainian music.

FESTIVALS

Lviv and Kyiv both host many festivals year round.

Lviv hosts about about 50 festivals around the city each year, most during peak tourist seasons. I highly recommend that you go to the **tourist information centre** to obtain a calendar of local events for the current week and month. In the first couple of months I was in Lviv, the city hosted its annual coffee festival, a nationally renowned yearly book fair, the Klezfest Jewish music festival, and a ballroom dancing competition on a small square nearby. Attending many of these events is free of charge.

Kyiv has also got its fair share of festivals, such as the Gogolfest, honouring writer Mykola Gogol, the Molodist Film Festival, a Beer Fest, a Medieval Battle Fest, and a wide range of other music, literary, cultural and folk fests.

ENJOY SOME TASTY UKRAINIAN FOOD

Ukraine's lengthy agrarian history, coupled with its rich, fertile, black *chornozem* soil has for centuries provided the nation with a large selection of incredibly tasty produce and a habit of eating well. Even most city dwellers are very knowledgeable about the seasonal produce calendar, the vitamin content and correct preparation of Ukraine's fruits of the soil. And most households will have a store of preserved berries, pickled vegetables, and dried fruit or mushrooms to last them through the winter.

One of the things I love most about living in Ukraine is the great food. When I first moved semi-permanently to Kyiv in my twenties and people would ask me why I was living there, I would often half jokingly reply, "the food". Honestly, though, out of all the places I have lived, Ukraine has been the easiest place to get a nutritious and tasty home-cooked meal for a very reasonable price in an easily accessible location. For full time young employees who don't have time to cook, this is a great advantage. Also, if you've ever tried Ukrainian dumplings (*varenyky*), beet soup (*borshch*) and cabbage rolls (*holubtsi*), you will probably understand why I was eager to enjoy these foods often.

Many inhabitants of Kyiv and Lviv take great pleasure in their dining and culinary experiences and would not want to waste money on a restaurant meal that was only sub-par. In turn, there are many restaurants that like to impress their customers with new dishes, seasonal menus and tasty treats, understanding that

Ukrainians expect meals cooked from scratch and made with fresh ingredients, which often even includes homemade drinks. In both cities, you will be able to choose from a wide variety of eating establishments, including both formal and casual restaurants, cafeteria style eateries, cafés and pubs that sell food, and street food. The main types of and most popular cuisines you will find are Italian, Japanese, Polish, Georgian and Jewish, and of course the must-try traditional Ukrainian dishes, and Ukrainian home style cooking (meat and potatoes type dishes with vegetables).

Salads are a big part of most menus, and many restaurants can list at least a dozen different options available. This vast selection of salads found in Ukrainian restaurants is something I often miss when eating out in Western Europe and North America. Common salads on Ukrainian menus include classic options such as Greek salad, Caesar salad with chicken and parmesan, shredded cabbage and carrot salad with seeds, a Ukrainian style vinaigrette, warm salads with veal or salmon and cherry tomatoes, and interesting combinations of warm beets and apple, walnuts and pears, shredded pumpkin and leeks, and a whole array of other options.

Many restaurants in Kyiv and Lviv also have impressive interiors, ranging from glam to minimalist modern to alternative-artsy styles, and use expensive furniture (no plastic chairs or tables), so eating out will be a quality and enjoyable experience. Sometimes even the bathrooms will be unique enough that they will be worth checking out, with interesting décor and use of mirrors, mosaics, and artwork.

In terms of food service, you might have to be open-minded, or better yet, direct in your expectations of the order in which you would like dishes served or in questioning wait times. Often Ukrainian dishes are brought to the table as soon as they have been prepared, but upon request, most restaurants are happy to bring food to all guests at the same time. Also please keep in mind that you will often have to order a side dish separately, as sides don't always come with a main meal. Also, the weight of a dish is still often provided on menus in grams. Many foreigners find this strange, but Ukrainians use these weights to judge how large the portions will be and sometimes to see if a meal is worth its price.

Nowadays, many people are more discerning about where their food comes, what pesticides may have been used on it and genetic modification. If those are concerns for you, you may have to be a bit more selective in your choices. With the relatively recent appearance of fast food in Ukraine, you might need to navigate a little to find the most amazing eateries and learn which fast food outlets and tourist traps to avoid. To ensure top quality, your best bet is to avoid places where food is heavily fried, and order meals made from seasonal vegetables, local dairy products, and meats such as local beef, rabbit, and quail, if that suits your tastes. Since 2009, Ukrainian law requires the labelling of GMO food, and most supermarket products have a *Bez GMO* (Without GMOs) label.

Drinks I can't mention restaurants in Ukraine without raving about the drink selection offered in most of them. Like the salad options, I am always impressed with the wide variety of non-alcoholic beverages, many of them natural, offered by many Ukrainian restaurants and cafés. Most places in Kyiv and Lviv offer freshly squeezed juices, which are very popular among the locals. Other popular choices in the summer are homemade lemonade, compote and *uzvar*. Compote is a warm or cooled lightly sweetened drink usually made from boiled berries, pears, or apples (a great alternative to juice), and *uzvar* is a drink made from dried fruit which usually has a bit of a smoky taste. Ukrainians also like a drink called *kvas,* which is dark, malty carbonated drink made from wheat, a sort of sweet non-alcoholic beer, which kids can drink. Lots of restaurants also offer high-quality fresh fruit juices made in Ukraine and the selection of herbal and green teas is also usually very good. Hot chocolate is often offered in two forms, as a milky "cocoa", or a thick, melted chocolate drink. As in most places in Europe, you will always find sparkling water on the menu and nice tasting bottled water. So if you don't drink caffeine, alcohol or sodas, you will probably delight in the drink options on Ukrainian menus.

Alcohol If you do drink alcohol, Lviv is a great place to try craft beer, Georgian wine, or the local pepper vodka served straight up in a shot glass and chased down with a thin slice of *salo* (pig fat) or cucumber. As drinking is an essential part of any social gathering involving friends and family, it naturally follows that alcohol is plentiful and freely available in Ukraine.

Beer drinkers are well served by popular brands such as Obolon, Chernihivske, Slavutych and Lvivske. The majority of beers are respectable lagers (*svitle*) found on tap in pubs and restaurants. Bottled beers are found in the street kiosks of Kyiv for less than 0.50 USD, and a half-liter in the pubs of Lviv will be around a dollar. Better beer is produced by independent microbreweries, for example, Kumpel, Pravda and Mons Pius in Lviv and Arena in Kyiv, who make interesting craft beer in a variety of styles. There is at least one brew pub or microbrewer in most larger Ukrainian cities. The darker, malted Bock-style beers (Dunkel or Porter), Imperial Stout and wheat beers (*bile*) tend to be more interesting and better quality than the lighter *svitle* or stronger *mitsne* lager styles.

Beer-drinking is often accompanied by pickled foods, dried fish and other hearty meat snacks. Thankfully, the ban on indoor smoking in restaurants and bars since 2012 has significantly improved the dining and drinking out experience for non-smokers.

Other popular national drinks include vodka (*horilka* in Ukrainian), which can be purchased in a range of qualities and flavours. Best advice is to stick to higher-priced, better known brands such as Nemiroff or Absolut. A half-decent bottle of vodka costs upwards from approximately $2 and is widely available in all supermarkets and smaller *produkty* grocery stores. Wine from Crimea is of variable quality but cheap and drinkable at the higher end of the price range with sparkling white wine (*champansky*) generally the most palatable. Better options are Moldovan wines which are good value and widely available in the larger supermarkets. Quality brandy or cognac, including that made in the Carpathian Mountains, is popular with older men. Western brands of all alcoholic drinks are freely available in most cities, especially in the more international restaurants and bars. And, yes, there are Irish pubs in Ukraine.

The main message is don't be shy to experiment and just go with the flow, especially if you find yourself toasting with vodkas at a special dinner. Drinking is a deeply rooted part of the Ukrainian culture and trying the local specialties is something you should not miss out on, even in moderation.

GET TO KNOW THE UKRAINIAN PEOPLE

The urban areas of Ukraine are full of impressive art, architecture, and historical monuments and the countryside is rich in unspoilt natural landscapes. In my opinion, however, it's really the people of Ukraine who make the country special. In general, they are welcoming, open-minded and helpful; their manners are European but, rather than being pretentious or uptight, Ukrainians, due to the challenging historical and economic situation, are for the most part refreshingly down-to-Earth and easy-going. Some visitors to Ukraine note that the locals maintain a balanced way of keeping up with current events and modern trends in fashion and technology while remaining rooted in the traditions and common sense ingrained in village life.

And despite the struggling economy and, often, hard life in Ukraine, you will probably be amazed at how educated Ukrainians strive to cultivate themselves and their children. It could be argued that it is precisely the hardship that makes Ukrainians determined to triumph over their circumstances. This includes always looking well-dressed (and made up for women) in public, having a nutritious diet, understanding the value of a good education, and pursuing many extra curricular activities which will develop them as people and bring more joy to their lives, such as dance classes, learning a musical instrument, chess, or sporting activities.

Ukrainians, particularly in Western Ukraine, appear to have very deep-rooted conventional European habits and very formal manners in public, which have been preserved in Ukraine over decades (whereas I notice that in Europe modernisation has accounted for some of these habits disappearing.) People are expected to behave very properly in public places (no shouting, throwing things, or getting rowdy) and children are meant to be polite and well-behaved. Men always shake hands with each other when meeting up and will often offer women their hand to help them off a tram. You will often see people putting newspapers or plastic bags down on a street bench or other outdoor seat before sitting down, to keep their clothes clean. The term "to be cultured" is used often by Ukrainians, as my 6 year-old daughter who attends school in Lviv often reminds me. In fact, many children's stories center around lessons on proper behaviour. We have one about an uncultured hippo who needs to learn proper   theatre etiquette, including being punctual, donning the proper attire, and refraining from looking at audience members with his binoculars.

On the other hand, considering Ukraine is a country of contrasts, you can also unfortunately sometimes see the opposite, "uncultured behaviour", such as men spitting on streets, swearing, public drunkenness (even in the morning), people leaving or throwing their trash on the streets and dog owners not picking up after their pets. To me there has always seemed to be two distinct categories of Ukrainians, or two sides to Ukraine: the side of high culture, good manners and education, in which my Ukrainian friends and I were raised, and the other of crime, a lack of respect for others and the environment, and "unculture". But perhaps this is so in every country.

According to UNESCO data, in 2015 the literacy rate in Ukraine was almost 100%. During the Soviet era, the majority of the population was expected to have a university education and this is still highly valued. The primary education system remains quite heavily based on rote-learning with a focus on memorising oodles of somewhat practical information and ensuring that all work is neatly handwritten and free of mistakes. How effective this system is, is a question for debate and in my mind it really depends on the course of study. What I have always noticed though, is that Ukrainians seem well grounded in basic knowledge and are able to converse on a wide range of topics, making them interesting interlocutors. This also means that at times they can tend to overestimate their level of expertise in a given area and might give the impression of being "know-it-alls".

To me, something which is sorely lacking in the national curriculum and way of life is the cultivation of respect for the environment. Though many citizens recognize the need for better waste management and recycling programs, an effective system has yet to be implemented. As a result, you may encounter unsightly and disorganized neighbourhood trash collection areas, or litter left in parks or forests. It seems that the Ukrainians' traditional connection to the Earth has not faired well in adapting to the realities of modernization and the convenience of plastic packaging.

Because Ukraine is relatively ethnically homogeneous, there is a common culture, religion and general feeling of unity among the people. Perhaps this is why approaching strangers is so easy and acceptable. On several occasions, a stranger has offered to hold my young child on her lap on a crowded bus, which is a completely safe and kind act.

At get-togethers you will appreciate the generosity and culture of inclusivity of the people you are with. There will be a lot of laughter, sharing of jokes, toasts, offering of food, pouring drinks for each other (pouring your own drink is considered a *faux pas*), and, at the end of the evening, leaving together or heading home in groups. At parties and weddings, Ukrainians are fond of organized activities and games and most seem to have no inhibitions at taking part. Nor do they with experimenting with interesting moves on the dance floor for that matter.

It is interesting to note that Ukrainians are generally more group oriented than individualistic (due probably to Ukraine's communist past), though this is also slowly changing. For example, as a student I took a train with a group of scouts to attend a weekend event. When I asked what to bring with me, one of the items was "snacks for the train", so I went out and bought individual portions of what I wanted to eat. After the train started moving, everyone pulled out their bulk portioned snacks, opened them and put them on the table so that anyone could share. The banana I had brought (among other snacks) turned out to be a bad option.

Though there is generally a collectivist mentality, when problematic issues arise, individual circumstances are often considered, rather than applying a set rule to a given situation. For example, in many jobs it is acceptable and easily forgive-able to be late for work if you were, for example, nursing your baby, or there was a traffic accident on your route to work, or simply that you were busy with another matter. Also, if you forget your ticket or pass to a venue (such as your student ID for transport), it is often possible to plead or negotiate entrance without it.

Ukrainians pride themselves on being freedom loving individuals and historical examples from *kozak*

(Cossack) times are often cited to illustrate this view. Perhaps this is why some have such difficulty in completely sticking to rules. Pushing ahead in line, asking for exceptions to be made, and taking extra time off work, are examples of this. From my experience, most Ukrainians don't like to be placed within strict boundaries. There is even some historical evidence that seems to support this. The French architect Guillaume Le Vasseur de Beauplan, who spent time in Ukraine from 1630 to 1647, made these interesting observations:

"They [Ukrainaians] are quick and intelligent. They are extremely witty and generous, they do not seek wealth. Instead, above all they value their freedom without which they do not want to live. There are no other Christian nations who think so little about the future as Ukrainians. And ... they are skilled in many trades... they are all quite smart, but particularly in those affairs that they consider useful and necessary, mainly that which is related to their village life. It is enough for them when they have enough to eat and drink."

Despite the many years of forced atheism in the Soviet Union, many people's beliefs generally remained strong, though hidden from public view, in most areas of Ukraine, particularly in the villages. Religion in Ukraine is still widely practiced and according to a 2003 Razumkov Center study, 75% stated a belief in God and 37% attended church on a regular basis. Aside from Western Ukrainians, not all attend Sunday mass regularly. There are also traditions stemming from pagan times which are still practiced, such as jumping over bonfires at the Ivana Kupala summer solstice, fortune telling on St Andrew's day or singing ancient New Year's songs related to nature. Also, certain individuals are believed to have special healing powers, or black magic. Babies are often still protected from "bad eyes" by closing windows at night, shielded from being looked at by strangers before they are baptised or protected from bad spirits by tying a red string around their wrists.

Some of the age-old celebratory traditions are amazing to witness in modern Ukraine. After Orthodox Christmas, young people walk around in groups, dressed in finely embroidered traditional costumes, beautifully and artistically singing Christmas and New Year's carols, elaborately reciting poems or taking on traditional roles such as that of Herod, the Three Kings, or the Goat (who traditionally represented the god of fertility). Another example is one of my favourite Spring holidays called "Wet Monday" (Easter Monday), when unsuspecting people are doused with water to symbolise cleansing. In Western Ukraine the girls know it is best to stay indoors on this day.

Many hard-working Ukrainians are understandably disgusted and deeply disappointed with the misappropriation of government funds and high-level corruption (the height of which was the billions of dollars stolen by ex-president V. Yanukovych, who is now in hiding in Russia), which has meant low wages for most of them and widespread poverty in many areas of the country. On top of that, Russia's annexation of Crimea and the subsequent war for control of Eastern provinces caused currency devaluation and inflation rates to soar. When you see well dressed respectable people enjoying a coffee or a meal in a local restaurant in Lviv you tend to wonder how they can afford to live on the average salary of $100-200 a month.

Some tips on Ukrainian etiquette...

Below is a brief, far from extensive list on Ukrainian etiquette or social norms which are good to be aware of:

It is very common to:

- wash your hands as soon as you enter someone's home.

- put on slippers when you enter your own or someone else's home; most people do not wear shoes inside, in order to keep apartments clean.

- bring something to the hosts if you are invited to someone's place. If there are children it is common to bring sweets, fruit, or a small gift for the children.

- when in a theatre, move down the aisle facing the people seated (it is considered rude to show them your backside).

- dress respectably (the frequent appearance of short skirts or sheer tops on women are accepted exceptions).

- say lengthy toasts at parties. Be aware that often foreigners are also invited to stand up and say a toast to the party host(s).

Please note that punctuality is not a universally valued trait in Ukraine. Though while some Ukrainians pride themselves on being on time, I grew up knowing that "being on Ukrainian time" meant being late.

Gender roles and Gallantry

You should also be aware that Ukrainians have very set gender roles, and this includes often referring to men as the "stronger" gender and women as the "beautiful" (but liberated) gender. Thought this is slowly changing, most Ukrainians are not at all bothered by this and believe that men and women have unique sets of traits that are complimentary to each other. Many take pride in their abilities to uphold their gender expectations, with women expressing their femininity though clothing styles, and striving to be good mothers, cooks and household managers, and men being the ones to carry heavy things, pay in supermarkets, fix the family car, and fulfill any other stereotypical male duties. It is commonly noted that men are meant to have the appearance of being the head of the household, but in reality, often the women are in charge.

In public, women are shown a lot of respect, and the hard work and efforts put forth by mothers and grandmothers are widely acknowledged. If women are out alone with their children, they will always be assisted and often offered a spot at the front of a line.

That said, there are many instances in Ukraine where too much of the family responsibilities are expected to be done by the woman and not as a "team effort", and where women feel oppressed or sexually harassed by men, which is one reason some Ukrainian women prefer to seek marriages with Western men.

Despite these tendencies, some marriages are equal partnerships, and most of my female friends in Kyiv are confident career women who employ nannies and/or housekeepers. Most would not consider the idea of being stay at home mothers (other than during infancy and breastfeeding stages), nor would they tolerate being treated with disrespect by their husbands.

Men in Ukraine usually:

-help women carry heavy bags
-offer a hand to women coming out of cars or off of trams or trains
-let women go through doors first
-pay for a woman's meal or ticket to a performance
-make way for a women with children to go to the front of a line

Also note that it is not common for Ukrainian women to shake hands when they meet someone (apparently it is not considered feminine), though nowadays some may be used to doing so with foreigners.

Nightclubs and casinos

From my experience, the nightclub scene in Ukraine can be seedy, expensive, exploitative for locals and targeted at taking advantage of foreigners. Many locals tend to socialise in restaurants, cafés or bars with live music and less often, at nightclubs with a group of friends. If you do go to a nightclub, be careful with meeting people. It's probably better to approach someone in a café, restaurant, park, museum, or even on the street than a nightclub. That said, *Picasso* in Lviv and *Arena* in Kyiv are known for featuring talented DJs.

UKRAINE FOR FAMILIES

Navigating Ukrainian cities with children in tow is not as smooth an experience as in other places, particularly with a stroller. But the number of family-friendly eateries and activities is steadily increasing, and so with the right planning and resources, Ukraine can be a great place for families to explore. You will notice many children out with their parents.

At airports, families will be invited to skip to the front of various queues. Nursing mothers are usually always given priority, even in official institutions.

As mentioned, if a mother is out with small kids, passers-by will offer assistance getting strollers into shops, up steps, or on and off public transportation. Strangers will often talk to and smile at your children wherever you go. Be aware that strangers may even offer your children sweets.

In Kyiv or Lviv, many working mothers hire nannies. For short term stays, some hotels may be able to offer child care or nanny services upon request.

You might want to avoid taxis if you are insistent on having working seatbelts and car seats; or make the effort to find a taxi that has them. You can ask your hotel to arrange this or inquire into VIP taxi services.

Note that due to Ukrainians' general concern for health, strangers might offer unsolicited advice in this area. Older ladies love to advise on how to dress your child for the weather, particularly if they see him/her without a hat on a windy day.

Lviv with Kids

From my experience, Lviv offers a great city holiday for kids, because of the walkability and activities for kids over 4. However, planning ahead and being aware of child-friendly activities is essential.

Kyiv with Kids

The centre of Kyiv has some great parks, but busy streets and crowded metros make it more difficult to get around with kids. The best options are child friendly cafes, or finding accommodation outside of the city centre. Most apartment buildings have outdoor playgrounds.

Turn to the Kyiv or Lviv city guides in Part II for more information on family-friendly venues.

UKRAINIAN FASHION AND BEAUTY

I think that most people who visit Ukraine for the first time quickly notice how strikingly beautiful the women are. Ukrainian women pride themselves on taking care of their outer appearance, and, as you stroll along the streets of any Ukrainian city, you might catch yourself wondering how there can be so many would-be models all around. I can't say for certain how the majority of Ukrainian women are able to have such a good sense of aesthetics or ability to put together fashionable outfits, but I chalk it up to the beauty of the embroidered national costume, a tradition in beautiful feminine dress passed down throughout the generations.

If they have the money and the time, Ukrainian women like to frequent salons for all their hair and nail needs; and due to the high demand for services, there is a salon every few blocks, and prices are quite reasonable. Whenever I come to Ukraine, I like to at least have a pedicure and haircut, because I know they will do a great job. (In fact, many Ukrainian women who move abroad complain that they can't find decent hairstylists or manicurists in their new country.) If you have more time, Ukrainian salons are also good at the following: hair colouring, eyebrow shaping and dying, waxing, and facials. Of course, for hygienic reasons, choose a salon that aspires to Western standards.

Note that complimenting women (or men), particularly on one's outer appearance, is very common in the workplace with most recipients feeling genuinely flattered by the attention.

UNIQUE UKRAINIAN EXPERIENCES

Lviv Shevchenkivskyi Hai

THINGS TO TRY

Something else I appreciate about Ukraine are the many unique experiences to be had here, some of them literally making you feel as though you've stepped back in time. Like visiting somebody in a village house which has no running water. Or taking a ride on a Communist era Lviv tram (some dating back to the 1950s) with older people dressed in the same classic clothing styles which also might have been popular 50 years ago. Some of these eye-opening experiences might take you out of your comfort zone, but they can also help to gain an appreciation for a way of life known to many Ukrainians.

Below is a list of a few unique Ukrainian experiences to try. If you are working with a travel agency or have a contact in the city you are going to, it is best to set up some of the following options in advance, because it might take 1-3 weeks to find the right onsite contact for you.

Try a banya Many Ukrainians like to go as a group to a sauna or a banya to relax. In traditional steam banyas, you have the option of being beaten ('massaged') with dried branches, wearing a felt hat, and then jumping into a cold pool, to get your circulation going.

Take a trip to a ghost city Many tourists are keen on visiting the "ghost cities" near the abandoned Chronobyl nuclear power station. Several tour companies specialize in trips to these spots. Use your own discretion in determining how safe the levels of radiation are.

Visit ornate churches Many of Ukraine's golden domed churches hold mass every day of the week and are open to visitors. In Orthodox churches women may be asked to wear a headscarf. Photographs of the stunning churches will provide beautiful memories of your trip.

Observe a tradition with pagan roots If you happen to be in Ukraine on July 6, you might be able to experience a traditional Midsummer's Eve with rituals such as wreath-making and searching for magical herbs. On January 19th, you might see people jumping into ice holes, or see fortune telling on Dec 13. After Easter you might also see young women in traditional dress singing lovely ancient Easter songs in either

Pyrohovo or Shevchenkivskyi Hai, two open air museums.

Host your special event in Ukraine If you'd like to try celebrating a special event in a memorable place, like an anniversary, birthday, wedding, or first solo concert, Ukraine is a great option. The catering, flowers, alcohol, and transportation are all very affordable, but what makes it most worth it are the beautiful or unique backdrops for your photos, and the fun that your Ukrainian guests or Ukrainian MC can provide.

Take the Lviv tram Board a number 2 tram on Rynok Square and go for a ride in either direction. Going east takes you down Lychakivska Street to the famous Lychakiv cemetery and the park *"Pohulyanka"*. The *Shevchenkivskyi Hai* Open Air Museum is also near the end of the line. Travel in the opposite direction and enjoy the 19th and early 20th century architecture from your window as your tram weaves through cobblestone streets. Just hop off at the last stop and go back in the other direction. The current tram fare is 2 UAH (about 8 cents US).

Visit someone in a village In order to do this, it's best if you know someone who comes from a village or who has friends or relatives living in a village, or check with one of the tour companies. You might catch a glimpse of some old style horse-drawn carriages, wooden churches, old-fashioned farm tools, or abacuses used in village shops. Village dwellers are usually very friendly and from my experience, love hosting visitors from outside of Ukraine. They are usually very generous with offering a meal and drinks, often insisting that you keep piling food onto your plate. It's a good idea to bring along a gift to be able repay their kindness in some way.

Leave the city If you can't manage or don't have time to visit someone in a village, it's a great idea to just travel to the nearest settlement outside a big city (difficult in Kyiv but also possible), to see Ukrainian nature and walk down some rural streets. I would highly advise taking the trip with a local friend since it might be hard to find English speakers or even to locate transport for your return journey.

Visit a castle or fortress As described in the Lviv section, some Lviv based tour companies offer trips to castles around Lviv. There are several other interesting castles and fortresses around Ukraine.

Take a train to another city Taking a train can often be a very interesting experience and a good glimpse at real life in Ukraine. On most trains, there are three categories of tickets – *lux* class, a two person "luxury" compartment (a 2 berth coupé), *KUPE* (coupé), a four person sleeping compartment (four berth coupé) with lockable doors, or *platzkart /platskarta*, an open plan wagon with benches/beds. The most authentic experience will be in *platzkart*, and chances are you will see Ukrainians pulling out and sharing containers of food, drinking beer together, playing cards or just chatting once the journey gets under way. You can usually purchase water, beer, tea, crackers or cookies from the train conductor.

Night trains are used for most travel across the country or between Kyiv and Lviv and all tickets sold will be for sleeping cars. In a coupé compartment, if you are travelling with people of both genders, when night-time hits, it is likely that the men will be asked to wait outside while the women change into their sleeping clothes (generally not pyjamas, but leggings or sweat pants) and vice versa. Before the train arrives in the morning, there will be a queue for the WC. The conductor will usually walk from berth to berth to take orders for tea, which most passengers will choose to order.

Please be warned that the toilet experience on most Ukrainian trains will not be pleasant. Not only are the seats metal and dirty looking, but the train jolts back and forth and side to side fairly violently adding further stress to the experience. If this is a problem for you, stick to the 6-hour new Hyundai "express trains" running between Kyiv and Lviv for more comfort.

Head to the mountains The Carpathian Mountains are breathtaking and great for camping and hiking in the summer, and for sledding in the winter. There are a few small but popular ski resorts, the largest of which, Bukovel, has greatly expanded its pistes, with prices and services now close to those of Western European resorts. After skiing or sledding you can enjoy a mulled wine or a cool or warmed spiced beer with a hot dish of stodgy mountain food.

Go to the seaside Many Ukrainians used to travel to Crimea every summer for a beach holiday, but this is not longer possible due to Russia's illegal annexation of the peninsula in 2014. You can still have a beach holiday in Ukraine though, in Odesa or Kherson.

Volunteer If you are interested in doing volunteer work, Ukraine can be a very rewarding place to do this. There are many people in need of assistance who would be extremely grateful to have help. Ideas for volunteer work include: teaching English in a local school or orphanage, helping the disabled or elderly, or being an elections observer. Americans can volunteer with the Peace Corps. You can also check out Volunteers for Peace, linked to UNESCO, and the Ukrainian Red Cross.

HERE ARE SOME OTHER OPPORTUNITIES THAT ARE QUITE EASY AND INEXPENSIVE TO ORGANISE IN UKRAINE:

Hobby lessons

In Ukraine it is very common to hire teachers to come to your home and teach you or your children a variety of skills including: playing an instrument, voice lessons, dance lessons (not as common), drawing/painting lessons, chess, photography, or languages. Cooking classes for groups have also become popular. Is there a particular hobby or language that you've always wanted to try learning but never gotten around to it or had the resources? If so, you can probably arrange a "test lesson" or a series of lessons during your stay. Be aware that finding the right teacher or fit might take a few weeks, but if you are coming for a short period of time you can probably arrange the classes before you arrive.

Get your dental work done

If your current health care plan doesn't cover dental work, then consider having a dental cleaning or other dental work done in Ukraine. There are now many clinics offering services equal to those abroad, for a much more affordable rate. And what I really appreciate is that I always seem to be able to make a last minute appointment either on the day I call or within a couple of days. I would say it is safe to drop into a modern looking dental clinic, and if you like what you see, book an appointment. I have had cavities filled and molars extracted with no issues or complications. In Lviv my family has gone to *Kohut and Kohut* and been very happy with their services.

Get anything repaired

Due to the economic situation, Ukrainians tend to repair their shoes, umbrellas, computers, phones, belts, glasses, or anything else in need of fixing rather than buy a newer model. The most popular repair shops are for shoes (getting new heels/soles), watches and jewelry, umbrellas and electronics. So if you have a collection of things at home that you would like to repair, you can bring them to Ukraine and you should be able to get them fixed quickly and cheaply.

Have a photo shoot

Ukrainians love taking photographs of themselves and their loved ones; you might notice in particular how they like to pose for photographs, ensuring a flattering take. You might want to try having a memorable photo shoot with your family or group of friends. You can try Googling for a local photographer.

Personal trainer in your home

My friends and I have had personal training sessions at home including yoga, pilates, dance, and weight training. Just be aware that you will have to provide any necessary equipment. You can either look for someone who speaks English, or try to make due with gestures and whatever languages skills either of you has. In Ukraine is that you are not expected to commit right off the bat, and can negotiate any agreements directly with the teacher.

Personal cook

If you like to know where the ingredients in your food come from, or if you like food to be prepared in a particular way e.g. gluten free or vegetarian, another amazing option is to be able to hire someone to come and cook in your own home or apartment, at a very affordable price (currently, about $10 for 4-5 hours spent preparing a few dishes). To find a cook, you may either ask your guide or translator, or call an agency. Be aware that the agency will also take a fee. It's best to ask a Ukrainian speaker to work out the details before you commit. You might also try Googling the following phrase "Домашній персонал Львів / Київ"

(household personnel in Lviv/Kyiv)

Get anything done

In Ukraine it often seems as though anything is possible, if you have the will and the money to pay for it (unfortunately sometimes in the form of "gifts" or bribes in government institutions), but often just on mutually agreed terms.

What I find most helpful is that people are flexible, often responding "Yes, we can make an agreement on that" to inquiries regarding personal services. Do you want to have a haircut at your home at 9pm or have an early morning photo shoot? Need someone to drive you somewhere? Turn a family photo into a painted portrait? Have a specific dress design sewn to your measurements? People are always looking for ways to make a bit of extra money, and so these types of services can often be set up. If properly arranged, you can also have many things delivered to your home for a fee.

A friend of mine manages a language agency in Kyiv and seems to be constantly innovating her business by quickly whipping up newly published materials and products or involving individuals from other fields (like art, cooking or Science) to spice up the language lessons. She seems to have no trouble finding the people and resources to put her ideas into action.

LEARNING ABOUT UKRAINIAN BELIEFS

If you speak English in Ukraine, chances are that the people you will end up meeting and speaking English with will have a university degree, and these educated people will be those from whom you will learn about the Ukrainian mentality and beliefs. Some common practices in Ukraine may strike you as odd, whereas others may seem sensible and might inspire you to re-evaluate your own habits.

COMMON UKRAINIAN BELIEFS

1) Health is of utmost importance. You will witness behaviour which accompanies this belief on a very regular basis. To Ukrainians, staying healthy often includes:

- Dress warmly on cold days, which in winter includes a proper hat, gloves, definitely something covering your lower back (long jacket or tucked in long top), tights or thermals underneath trousers for people of all ages, and warm boots (you can buy sheepskin insoles for the winter months). You may find it surprising on spring days to see children dressed to protect every inch of their bodies from being exposed to cold air or a draught. In Ukraine there is a strong belief that if cold air blows on a part of the body, such as you tailbone, ears, or back, you can "chill" it, leading to inflammation).

- **Never, ever sit on cold pavement** or other cold surfaces, as, according to Ukrainians, your rear end will catch a chill, leading to a bedridden illness. If you want to experiment, try sitting on pavement and wait to see how many passers-by give you disapproving looks or tell you to stand up.

- **Ukrainians believe in eating soup before lunch** to "line their stomachs".

- **If a Ukrainian falls ill, s/he does not go into work**. This is based on the logical, down-to-earth notion of resting when you are ill and not pushing and overly medicating yourself though an illness.

- **Most Ukrainians are deathly scared of catching a cold from draughts** and will make sure that when windows are open in a room, the doors are shut; also, windows will often remain closed on public transport on hot summer days.

- Despite the focus on health, sweet snacks, chocolate and cake are frequently consumed by the majority of Ukrainians, and fried foods and sweet drinks are common at the dinner table.

2) Also somewhat related to number one: **spine and back health is very important.** This is why children are repeatedly told to sit up very straight at their desks at school and are constantly encouraged to stand tall. Paediatric appointments before entry into school include an examination of the spine (as well as foot formation, vision, teeth, a stool sample and an interview with a neurologist). If even minor deviations are found within the spine or neck, regular massages, swimming, gymnastics or dance classes will be recommended.

3) It is very important to be well-read and knowledgeable. In Soviet times, children and teens were given a yearly list of literature to read over the 3 month summer holidays, including classics such as *War and Peace* and *Crime and Punishment*.

4) Be loyal to your friends and family. Loyalty is very important and it is usually taken as a given that you will go out of your way to help your close friend or relative if s/he is in need of assistance. This may include lending money to relatives or offering "favours" if you have an official job in a government or tax office, at a railway station or other official institution.

5) Love for one's country is a big part of the Ukrainian identity, particularly in central and western Ukraine, and particularly since the 2014 Revolution of Dignity. Ukrainians are very proud of their national cuisine, beautiful women, folk songs, their rich history, and their ability to make do with only minimal resources.

6) Most Ukrainians believe that the ultimate outcome of any situation is up to God. A common response to questions relating to the future is "*Yakshcho dast Boh*", which means "God-willing".

7) **It is customary to speak directly to people and not hide your feelings behind pleasantries** (i.e. what other cultures might feel is "being polite"). Ukrainians believe that if you are not happy about something you need to let others know, otherwise you are not being honest and no one can tell what you really want or need.

8) **Generosity and sharing is important.** Children are instructed to not be "жадібний" or "жадний" (greedy) with their toys.

9) **Sometimes it is necessary to endure unpleasant physical or emotional pain in order to achieve your end goal.** In these situations, and those merely requiring patience, children are told from a young age "потерпи" (*poterpy*) which roughly translated to "endure it" or "just deal with it".

INTERESTING FACTS ABOUT UKRAINE and UKRAINIANS

1) *Carol of the Bells* was originally composed by Ukrainian composer Mykola Leontovych in 1914. The original lyrics are based on a Ukrainian folk chant welcoming in the New Year.

2) Ukraine had **one of Europe's first Constitutions**, published in 1710 by Pylyp Orlyk, which democratically separated powers between legislative, judicial and executive branches of government and appeared almost 40 years before Montesquieu's *Spirit of the Laws*.

3) During the times of **Kyivan Rus'** (9-13th century), Ukraine's capital Kyiv was home to **one of the most powerful states** in Europe.

4) **Anna of Kyiv** (daughter of Grand Prince Yaroslav the Wise) **married French King Henry I** and after his death ruled France until her son Philip came of age. She was literate (rare in the 11th century) and her signature in Ukrainian appears on a French government document from that time.

5) It was Kyiv-born Igor Sikorsky who designed the **first helicopter** in 1939.

6) The **modern kerosene lamp** was invented in Lviv in 1853. In fact there is a monument in Lviv to inventors Lukasevych and Zech on Virmenska Street.

7) You probably know that Ukraine was once known as the "breadbasket of Europe". But did you know that the yellow portion of the **Ukrainian flag** symbolises the fields of wheat? The blue represents the sky.

8) Kyiv's Arsenalna metro station is the **deepest metro station in the world**.

9) The **longest wind instrument in the world** is the Trembita, a 3-4 meter long alpine horn instrument traditionally used in the Carpathian Mountains.

10) Ukraine once had the **third largest nuclear arsenal** in the world, but voluntarily handed everything over to Russia in 1996 in exchange for Russia's promise to protect Ukraine's sovereignty.

Now that you have had a general overview of some of the great things to be found in Ukraine, below are mini city guides for specific attractions and restaurants to be found in Lviv and Kyiv, as of the time of publishing.

PART II - LVIV AND KYIV CITY GUIDES

LVIV

LVIV HOTELS

The number of hotels in Lviv has greatly risen since hosting the Fifa Euro 2012 Soccer Championship and you will find a large selection of hotels and hostels for different budgets. Here are a few we have tried and liked:

Chopin Hotel is a few minutes' walk from Rynok Square and is located on a quiet street across from a small square. They have a nice terrace restaurant at the back of their hotel.

We enjoyed our stay at the modern **Rudolfo** with minimalistic décor, located near *Ploshcha Rynok*. The staff are very friendly and helpful, and the breakfast is delicious. We appreciated the existence of an elevator after long days spent exploring Lviv on foot.

Leopolis Hotel is a more luxury boutique hotel with slightly higher prices located in a UNESCO world heritage site. Their basement spa, located in a renovated 19th century wine cellar, with its Jacuzzi, Finnish sauna and small gym are highly recommended.

On the Square Guesthouse is another great and affordable option, with beautifully renovated rooms reflecting the characteristic Austro Hungarian style.

Staying at the **George Hotel**, the oldest hotel in Lviv, built in 1901, offers a more authentic Ukrainian experience. The grand spacious staircase gives patrons a feel for the Lviv of Austro-Hugarian times. Rates are quite affordable.

Other recommendations are the **Swiss Hotel, Atlas DeLuxe**, and the **Vintage Boutique Hotel**, which offers an amazing brunch.

The new **Edem Resort and Spa**, a 30-minute journey from Lviv, offers a relaxing and luxurious spa break. Note that it is not open to families with children.

GREAT LVIV ATTRACTIONS

Lviv attractions; the "Wonder Train"

Below are some of the best tourist attractions in Lviv.

Independent Walking Tour There are so many interesting things to see walking around Lviv's city centre and it's very easy to get from one place to another, so you might choose to get your sightseeing started by wandering around by yourself admiring Lviv's nooks and crannies, beautiful historic buildings and impressive monuments.

Guided Walking Tours Many guides specialise in particular aspects of Lviv's rich history and can share a wealth of interesting stories and information about the city as you walk. You can find several options for guided walking tours on the Internet. Here are a few sites to get you started. *https://www.toursbylocals.com/Lviv-Tours*

http://chudotour.com.ua/en/excursions/lviv-bagatonacionalnii/

Custom or Guided Tours The Canadian tour company **Cobblestone Freeway** also offers great options for tours to Ukraine. You can organize a custom tour with their assistance, or join one of their scheduled tours such as the **Vocal Tour**, the **Folk Art and Culture Tour**, the **Photography Journey** and more. They even offer family history tours for families with Ukrainian roots. *http://cobblestonefreeway.ca/destinations/ukraine/*

"Wonder Bus" large city tour (1.5 hours) If you'd like a tour of the wider city in the comfort of a bus, check out the Wonder Bus. *http://chudotour.com.ua/en/excursions/big-centre-wonder-bus/*

"Wonder Train" small city tour (1 hour) Travelling around the city in the Wonder Train is fun for adults and children alike. *http://chudotour.com.ua/en/excursions/the-small-centre-wonder-train/*

Cycling Tours - Inside the city These two companies offer cycling tours within the city limits: *http://bicyclerent.lviv.ua/en/index.php*

http://www.activeukraine.com/ukraine-tours-archive/lviv-parks-cycling-tour/

Cycling Tours - Outside the city This company offers cycling tours to the magnificent 14th -18th castles situated in the rural areas around the city of Lviv. *https://www.excursiopedia.com/en/tours/lviv-castles-cycling-tour-2382*

Lviv High Castle / Lviv Castle Hill Known by both names, this tourist attraction is the ruins of an ancient castle and the highest point in the city. If you are up for trekking uphill (about a 25 minute walk from the city centre), give it a try. Once you get to the top you will have a nice view of the city. There is a restaurant on the hill where you can have a drink or snack after your long walk.

Christmas Markets In December and January, wooden kiosks are set up in several parts of the city centre, which sell drinks, snacks and a wide variety of handmade goods (such as wool socks, mitts and vests, toys, cloth or wooden Christmas decorations) and kitschy souvenirs. Along Ruska Street the new bar "The Drunk Cherry", is hugely popular and always packed with people standing around high tables enjoying a glass or two of cherry liqueur.

Skating Rink During the winter months you can also rent skates at the skating rink located on Market Square. I would advise to avoid going on Sunday afternoons when the rink can get crowded.

The Coffee Mine This is a café with a free tourist attraction in the basement. After you enjoy your coffee, you can head downstairs and check out the "mine", where the café jokingly claims they extract their own coffee beans. This is fun for children and adults alike. There is also an enclosed courtyard serving beer in addition to their coffee, which offers live music some evenings. Many people like to purchase Coffee Mine coffee beans as a gift for friends back home.

The Italian Courtyard For a small entrance fee, you can visit Lviv's only "Italian courtyard", located across from city hall, and have a coffee or meal while you admire the beautiful architecture.

Lviv's Churches Ukraine has many beautiful ch
While walking around the centre of Lviv, th
several that you can visit, including the Dominican
Sobor, the stunningly ornate Boyim Chapel (built in
1615), St Andrew's Church, the Armenian Cathedral
and more.

The Potocki Palace This building is another of Lviv's
architectural gems, built in Baroque style in the 1880s.
Today it is used both as part of the next-door Lviv Art
Palace, and for official meetings of the President of
Ukraine when he is in Lviv.

Vernissage Outdoor Arts Market Located on
Teatralna street just down from the Opera theatre, the
"Vernissage" is the best place in Lviv to buy
embroidery, Ukrainian folk crafts, T-shirts, and
souvenirs. Many of the sellers are from rural regions
of Western Ukraine and have made their crafts
(particularly embroidered cloths) by hand. You can
also purchase amateur paintings, many of which
feature Lviv street scenes.

**Lviv's First Phramacy "Apteka" Museum "Under the
Black Hawk"** This is the oldest existing pharmacy in
the city of Lviv as it has been around since 1774. Entry
into the first room of the still working pharmacy is free;
in it you will see historical elements such as hundred-
year-old mixing bowls and chests of drawers with the
names of medicines written in Latin. For about 1 USD
you can purchase a ticket to view the rest of the
pharmacy, including the basement and courtyard.
http://lvivpharmacy.org.ua/

D.S. Secret Pharmacy is a second historical pharmacy-museum offering tours daily from 10am to 8pm. They have an English language website. The pharmacy was discovered in 2012 during renovations, when a hidden door was found and opened. *http://secret.lviv.ua/en/*

Masoch café Did you know that Lviv is where the term masochism originated? The author Leopold von Sacher-Masoch, born in 1836 in Lviv to an Austrian father and Ukrainian mother, is famous for writing novels expressing his masochistic fantasies. There is an interactive monument to Masoch (check for a surprise in his pocket!) in front of the café bearing his name. It all makes for a favourite photo spot for tourists. Though named a café, it seems to function more as a bar, open daily from 12pm to 4am, and with the interior and menu living up to the Masoch name.

Kryivka Restaurant This theme restaurant, one of many which Lviv seems to pride itself on, is very popular among tourists, not necessarily for the food, but for its unique atmosphere. The restaurant is decorated to simulate an underground hideout/bunker (aka *kryivka*) of the Ukrainian Insurgent Army (UPA) from WWII. Though the UPA army had a complex history, the patrons of this restaurant are just interested in the fun of the experience. A man holding a Kalashnikov requests a secret password as he greets customers at the door, and if correct, he offers a shot of vodka to be downed before actually being seated. Be aware that during the high season the line up to get in can be very long. *https://www.facebook.com/kryjivkalviv/*

Castle tour around Lviv The castle tour mentioned above can also be reached by bus or private car. The link below provides one option for an organized trip. *http://www.inlviv.info/services/castles_tour/*

Shevchenkivskyi Hai Open Air Museum If you would like to get a feel for the romantic Ukrainian village life of the past, then Shevenkivskyi Hai is the place to go, with its quaint clay houses, elaborate wooden churches and role players in traditional dress. There is an outdoor restaurant where you can sample Ukrainian dishes such as *varenyky* and *borshch*. Next to the restaurant you can try your hand at archery with the assistance of a kozak in traditional clothing. You can also take a ride on a horse drawn wagon. Sometimes classes like painting or doll making are offered for kids. *http://en.lvivskansen.org/*

LVIV ARTS & CULTURE

Lviv Museums
In addition to the pharmacy museums listed above, Lviv has a few other small museums in the centre, and some a little farther out.

First Post Office/ Bandinelli Palace This beautiful building, dating back to 1593, was Lviv's first post office and the home of Italian merchant Roberto Bandinelli. It lay in ruins for many years until it was restored and re-opened in 2005. The museum is a recreation of what the house may have looked like in that time, including cooking facilities and an adjacent dining room. *http://bandinelli-palace.virtual.ua/en/*

Museum of Glass The museum of glass is a small basement museum featuring a few displays of historical glassware (some from Roman colonies in Crimea from the 3rd century) and some modern glass art on display. They occasionally host glass making classes and even concerts. You can check their English language website for upcoming events. *http://www.glassmuseuminlviv.org/*

Public Zoological Museum of the Ivan Franko University It might be of interest to you to visit one of the oldest university museums in Europe, which features fauna from all over the world, including more than 180,000 artifacts (of which 10,000 are on exhibit). *http://zoomus.lviv.ua/en/*

Museum of Bread For a unique experience in the country, which was once known as the "breadbasket of Europe", pay a visit to the Bread Museum on Number

89, Pasichna Street. Though they don't have their own website, the following link has the address and phone number. Since it is out of the city centre, it's best to call ahead to make sure they are open. *http://www.karpaty.info/en/uk/lv/lw/lviv/museums/hliba/*

Museum of Beer Lviv prides itself on its centuries old beer-making history and has established a museum dedicated to this trade. The museum, which has ancient beer bottles and beer making recipes on display, is a short walk or tram ride (number 7) out of the city centre, but definitely an interesting attraction.

You may also arrange a tour (with beer tasting) of the adjacent Lviv Brewery, founded in 1715 (making it 300 years old), which began its cooperation with Carlsberg Ukraine in 1999. *http://en.carlsbergukraine.com/production/lv/*

Visual arts

While in Lviv you can admire or purchase Ukrainian paintings at one of the small art galleries or from collections hanging in restaurants or cafés. Ukrainian artwork is appealing for its use of vibrant colours and the beautiful renditions of Ukrainian village or nature scenes.

Lviv Art Galleries

Art Gallery of Madame Palmgren This art gallery located across from the Dominican church has a large collection of paintings and sculptures by talented artists from Lviv and elsewhere in Ukraine. Works are often bought by collectors living in North America or

Europe. *http://palmgren-gallery.com/en/*

Art Veles Gallery The Art Veles Gallery has a good selection of artwork by prominent Ukrainian artists, including paintings, sculptures, tapestries, glasswork, and artistic handicrafts. *http://artveles.com/*

Green Sofa This is another small art gallery where you can view or purchase Ukrainian painting, sculptures, and other artwork. *http://artgreensofa.com/?lang=en*

Lviv Art Palace (Palats Mystetstva) This art gallery, built in 1996, is the largest exhibition hall in Ukraine, with 12 exhibit rooms, the ceilings of some of which are 8 meters high. It is the venue of the Annual Publisher's Forum, a hugely popular event attended by book lovers from all over Ukraine. *http://lpm.com.ua/en*

Dzyga Situated at the end of the narrow Virmenska Street, Dzyga used to be a popular meeting spot for artists and writers, but much of its space has now been turned into a restaurant. There is a very small art gallery offering free admission to its exhibits. *http://dzyga.com/artgallery/en/teksty.html*

Lviv Art's online gallery You can also check out and purchase art by prominent Ukrainian artists at the following website of the Ukrainian online art gallery. *http://ukrainart.com/*

Yuriy Titovets Prostir Photo Gallery If you are interested in photography, this photo gallery is definitely worth a visit. It was created out of the conference room of Mr Titovets' dentistry office, who wanted to use the space in a more creative and intimate way. (I told you Ukrainians were creative!) It features the works of prominent Lviv photographers and the gallery also offers classes in photography.

Folk Art

I love admiring the richness and deep symbolism of Ukrainian embroidery, painted Easter eggs, tapestry, ceramics, woven straw and other traditional arts.

Many venues and gift shops will features these items. The best examples I have seen in Lviv are at the Vernissage arts market (though most are not historical items) and small exhibits which can be found in some of Lviv's museums.

Museum of Ethnography and Folk Art/Art Crafts This museum, located on two floors, has exhibits featuring century old house furnishings, national costume, dolls, and other rotating exhibits. *http://ethnology.lviv.ua/*

Andrey Sheptytskyi Lviv National Museum This prominent museum was established in 1905 by Archbishop Andrey Sheptytskyi. It is well worth a visit as it is one of the largest museums in Ukraine and hosts vast collections of artifacts related to Ukrainian culture, mostly icons and folk art. Kids might enjoy the collection of Ukrainian folk toys exhibited. *http://nm.lviv.ua/*

Performing Arts

There are many venues in Ukraine for attending plays, operas, ballets, concerts and other types of performing arts. For a list of upcoming performances (called AFISHA in Ukrainian), you can check with the Lviv tourist info centre or the Kyiv Weekly/Kyiv post newspapers. Keep in mind that most plays will be shown in Ukrainian; if you don't understand the words, you might still enjoy visiting a centuries old theatre and getting a feel for the Ukrainian theatre experience. If not, it's best to stick to the musical performances.

Lviv Opera Theatre

Lviv Theatre of Opera and Ballet Attending an opera or ballet is a must-do experience when visiting Lviv, and it's worth going to a show even just to admire the Opera theatre itself, which was built in 1900 using features of Renaissance and Baroque architecture. You can buy tickets right inside at the *Kasa* (ticket office), but make sure you turn up during ticket sales hours. You can also buy tickets online if you can work out the Ukrainian language ticket sales site. *http://opera.lviv.ua/en/*   Ticket sales: *https://gastroli.ua/*

Les Kurbas Lviv Academic Theatre If you are interested in experimental theatre, then this progressive theatre, created in 1988 by a group of young actors, is a great venue to check out. *http://en.kurbas.lviv.ua/*

Lesia Ukrainka Lviv Drama Theater The repertoire has long included writer Lesia Ukrainka's famous *Lisova pisnya* (Forest Song) play and other classical works by Ukrainian others. A list of other performances for both children and adults, ranging from Winnie the Pooh and Rikki Ticki Tavi to Dear Pamela by J. Patrick is available on their site. *http://ldt-ukrainky.lviv.ua/*

Maria Zankovetska National Drama Theatre This theatre, which had its first performance in 1842, was once one of the largest theatres in Europe. It features both traditional Ukrainian and modern international plays. Many of the actors hold the title of National and Honoured Artists of Ukraine. *http://www.zankovetska.com.ua/*

Lviv Philharmonic Lviv's philharmonic has a good selection of performances throughout the year, for adults as well as for children, including holiday-themed performances, jazz events, solo concerts, classical orchestra concerts and more. *http://www.philharmonia.lviv.ua/?setlang=en*

LVIV RESTAURANTS

There are so many great places to eat in Lviv and many online resources with customer's reviews for finding out about the restaurants; and new ones are popping up all the time. When you arrive in Ukraine you will most likely head out of your accommodation towards the centre and choose from whichever restaurant looks the best to you. However, I am happy to share a concise list of my favourite restaurants and cafés in Lviv and Kyiv.

For me, going out to eat in Lviv is an all around better experience with more original restaurants, more home-grown ingredients, better prices and all usually within walking distance of each other.

If you're looking for a good lunch deal, many restaurants offer a separate 'business lunch' menu, which you might need to request. Business lunch usually includes a small soup, salad, main course and dessert or drink. These are usually under 5 USD.

LVIV RESTAURANT RECOMMENDATIONS

Mons Pius The ancient courtyard and terrace of this restaurant is always packed on summer evenings, whilst the cozy, dark indoor wood panelled dining spaces are busier in the colder months. The tasty meals on offer are filling and delicious, using nice cuts of meat and vegetable based sides. Their own home brewed beer is a must-try and goes well with their beer snacks.

The Most Expensive Galician Restaurant Another bizarre entrance, through the kitchen of an old Lviv apartment, leads to a smart restaurant overlooking Market Square. With a meat-dominated menu, the joke prices are reflected in the extra zero added to each dish. Thankfully the food is good.

On Shevska Part of the Leopolis Hotel, this is a good value restaurant with an Italian/Mediterranean focus. Dining is casual in a smart but unfussy way, with excellent service.

Atlas Restaurant If you want to try some traditional Ukrainian *varenyky* at any time of day, or a good *borshch*, this is the place to go. Also, it's a great place to go for breakfast to enjoy an egg dish, crepe or cottage cheese pancakes, with a strong cappuccino. The business lunches are also amazing value.

Trapezna This restaurant is a little harder to find as it is in one of Lviv's trademark basement locations in a former monastery, but it is well worth searching for. The food is absolutely delicious including original dishes, such as walnut bean mash, onion pie, and rabbit stewed in sour cream, using ingredients that taste like they were just brought in from the garden.

Green Café It was exciting to discover this vegetarian/vegan café in Lviv at a time when we didn't think that such things existed here. They also offer gluten and dairy free options. We love the spinach smoothies, the original healthy dishes such as raw zucchini pasta with pesto, healthy raw nut based desserts and simple healthy foods for kids like boiled potatoes, buckwheat or veggie sticks with hummus.

Their menu changes seasonally.

Szkocka restaurant in Atlas Deluxe Hotel The restaurant of this luxury hotel offers a calm, classic interior, impeccable service, and tasty international/Ukrainian dishes for very reasonable prices. The business lunch, including a small salad, soup, small main dish and drink, is currently a steal at under $4.

Garmata Restaurant, Citadel Inn Perched above the city in a luxuriously converted fortress, the Garmata offers a high standard of cuisine in a calm and well-appointed restaurant with city views. In summer there is an open-air restaurant. Their meals are worth the uphill trek. The traditional **Amadeus** and **Veronika** stalwarts still have atmosphere but have lost their edge to worthy competitors.

For other recommendations of the many good restaurants to choose from in Lviv, turn to Google or a city guide such as: *http://lviv.travel/en/index/wheretoeat*

LVIV CAFES

Lviv's coffee tradition dates back to the late 17th century, when Lviv native Yuriy Kulczycki made the drink popular after having opened the first coffee house in Vienna. Lviv is proud to still consider itself the coffee capital of Ukraine, holding an annual coffee festival each fall. The centre of Lviv seems to have a café every few metres, and when the weather is warm, these cafés are always overflowing with locals and tourists alike. Though I have always noticed that the pace of work in Lviv seemed comparatively slow, before the tourist boom it still always used to surprise me to see so many people leisurely enjoying a cup of coffee on a regular work day. Below are my favourite Lviv cafés, based on the atmosphere and the quality of the coffee.

Coffee Manufacture A classic espresso or cappuccino at this café tastes great and this small, stylish chain offers a range of house blends of Arabica and Robusta. They also have flavoured coffee beans (i.e. rather than using syrups) including cherry, chocolate, Irish cream, nutmeg and more, all reasonably priced.

Lviv Chocolate Workshop If you're looking for a fun chocolatey coffee experience, then head over to the popular Lviv Chocolate Workshop on Serbska Street, just off the Market Square. Tourists flock there try their hot chocolate, which is a cupful of old fashioned thick, melted chocolate, and purchase chocolate gifts. Their chocolate latte is also a popular choice. For me the highlight of this location is the kids'/family room on the fourth floor. For less crowded locations in Lviv and other cities, please check their website, which I have listed in the kids activities section.

Bilka This is an amazing café to try if you're looking for something with a stylish, modern, minimalistic interior away from the crowds of tourists. It's located on the 4th floor of the Roksolana city centre mini mall next to the Halytskyi market and has a nice view of Lviv's St. Andrew's church. The coffee and teas are good and the scrumptious desserts include a chocolate-coconut brownie cake and one of the best cheesecakes in Lviv. My favourite breakfast dishes are the spinach and egg polenta and the gluten free zucchini pancakes. They also have a kids' corner with toys and drawing supplies.

Cukernia If you're looking for mouth watering cakes with a coffee on the side, then the hands down winner for us is Cukernia, with its delicious hand-made cakes and pastries. In the summer we usually order the heavenly tasting raspberry crème roll.

Svit Kavy This café offers the best combination of excellent coffee, heavenly desserts (such as their lemon meringue pie or the mint white chocolate macaroons), filling snack meals, and a classic, stylish interior. They also offer great breakfast options starting at 8:30.

There are certainly many other great cafes in Lviv; in fact there are just too many to list.

ACTIVITIES FOR KIDS IN LVIV

Indoor Kids' clubs

Lys Mykyta Located right off Market Square, this indoor play centre is a great place for kids to run off steam or engage in imaginative play. You can relax on bean bags as you watch your children, or drop them off and do some sightseeing. Please note that it is open from 11am until 9pm every day, and can get busy at the weekends. *http://lys-mykyta.org/*

Dyvokray is a slightly smaller alternative to Lys Mykyta, and is located just a few streets over in the Roksolana mini mall on the fourth floor. *http://www.roksolana.ua/дивокрай/*

Kuzya is an informal mini kindergarten. I have dropped my daughter off in the summer for small group lessons and activities. It is best for kids who have knowledge of Ukrainian as there are organised lessons between 10-2pm. *http://baby-center.lviv.ua/*

The toy store **Antoshka** on Prospekt Svobody, also has a large area where kids can play for free, and a café offering kid-friendly food.

Children's Theatres in Lviv

I am impressed that there are so many options for children and teens to enjoy performing arts in Lviv. With small children, it often doesn't matter what language the play they are watching is in.

Lviv Puppet Theatre This Soviet-era puppet theatre holds puppet shows almost daily and has over 200,000 viewers per year. The cost of a ticket is 20 UAH/ under 1 USD. *http://lvivtelesyk.com.ua/*

Lyalky i Lyudy This is a private puppet theatre in a renovated underground location, offering fun shows for kids. It also has shows almost daily. *http://www.puppet.lviv.ua/en*

First Ukrainian Theatre for Children and Youth (Teatr Yunoho Hlyadacha) This theatre presents creative renditions of children's stories or plays such as Cinderella, the Three Little Pigs, Oliver Twist, and some classic Ukrainian children's plays. We have been very impressed with the enthusiasm of the actors and the colourful, creative costumes. Depending on the seats chosen shows during the day cost between 16 and 22 UAH (under 1 USD). *http://nashteatr.lviv.ua/*

Arts and Crafts

Maister Klas / Master Class / Art lesson This is the term used for a very popular type of activity offered for children in Ukraine, particularly around holidays. It is basically any type of class for children lasting 1-2 hours as a way to teach them something new and keep them occupied. Often the classes are centred around an art activity, such as a unique painting technique, quilling, doll making, applique, candle making and more. These classes are usually offered by kids' clubs, museums, art galleries, cafes and restaurants.

Yurashky, the gingerbread shop offers master classes in baking or decorating gingerbread cookies and is a fun place for kids to visit.

Parks

"**Park Franka**" or "**Ivana Franka Park**" is located opposite the Ivan Franko National University, and is a great place to go for an afternoon of play in the fresh air. Besides strolling, scootering, or cycling along the hilly paths, kicking a ball around or squirrel watching, there is a relatively large playground with nice equipment. On weekends in the summer there are arts events and the traditional Ukrainian park activities involving trampolines, bouncy castles and pony rides.

If you want to venture farther out of the centre, there are a few other nice parks a few tram stops away from the centre. Two other options are **Park Kultury**, which has a ropes course for children, carousels and other rides, and the beautiful and vast

Stryjskyi Park, which has a children's train ride.

Shevchenkivskyi Hai described in the general Attractions section. This is our favourite kid friendly outing in Lviv. *http://lvivskansen.org/*

Swimming pools

Sofia Grand Club Fitness Centre (with pool) This small pool offers drop-in rates, individual and group lessons for adults and kids. *http://fitness-sofia.com/bass.html*

Lviv "Beach" Water Park The existing 1984 swimming complex was rebuilt in 2008 into a modern water park. It is the largest indoor water park in Western Ukraine. It has waterslides, a kid's pool, a 50-metre swimming pool, an outdoor area for tanning on sunny summer days and an adjoining restaurant. *http://www.aqualviv.com.ua/*

Other activities

Rides / Carousels For small children, there are small carousels set up outside the Opera house and in most of the parks that you can use for a fee.

Outdoor skating rink As mentioned, in the winter there is a skating rink directly on Market Square. You can rent skates but please be aware that there are no helmets available to rent. Again, I would advise not going on a Sunday when the rink may be crowded.

Circus If you are interested in seeing a traditional style circus show, check out the Lviv circus website for their current shows. *http://www.lvivcirk.com/*

Studios

Bila Pantera Dance Bila Pantera is a drop-in dance studio located outside the city centre. If you are up for the 15-minute bus ride or a short taxi journey, you can drop in or arrange for a private lesson. You can find their list of classes online, but please call ahead to make sure the class is a go-ahead on any particular day. *http://www.dance-lviv.com/*

Zhyrafa (Giraffe) is a yoga studio specializing in kids' yoga classes and those for children with disabilities. *http://girafa.lviv.ua/*

Private music lessons If your child is interested in trying out a musical instrument, or if you need practice while on holidays, you may be able to find a private music teacher. It is best to contact your tour guide (or an agency such as *http://www.activeukraine.com/request-custom-tour/* ahead of time to arrange it. Another source is the web site "repetitor.ua". *http://www.repetitor.ua/?lang=en*

Exhibits for kids

Museum of Nature This small museum, renovated and reopened in 2013 (giving it a more modern look) has a selection of fauna that can make for an interesting visit. They often have special exhibits for kids and presentations for school groups, like a bird exhibit at Easter time every year. Other exhibits feature rock, soils, insects, and animals. An adult ticket is 10 UAH and children over six pay 5 UAH. The museum has plans to expand in the coming years. *http://www.smnh.org/ua/*

Other museums Your children might enjoy exploring any of the other museums listed in the activities section, and often kids under 6 are free. I wouldn't recommend them for kids under 4 though, as there are many artefacts on open display that you might have to hold your child back from touching.

Malls

FORUM Mall This mall is just a short walk from the city centre and features a movie theatre with some English language films, a large toy shop, a food court and a children's play area called Ihroland.

King's Cross Mall You can take a local bus or a taxi to this large mall. In addition to a good selection of clothing stores and a food court, there is a skating rink, a bowling alley, an IMAX theatre, a 5D movie theatre, and a "Lazer Maze". *http://www.kingcross.com.ua/en/entertainment/*

LVIV CAFES AND RESTAURANTS WITH PLAY AREAS

Maisternia Shokoladu (Lviv Chocolate Factory) As mentioned above, the location on Serbska Street has a family room on the fourth floor with a selection of toys, a play house, bean bags, and a large TV playing cartoons. You are asked to take off your shoes in the family room, making it a clean place for kids to play on the floor. The bathroom next door has an item rarely found in Ukrainian toilets, a baby change table.

Miaso i spravedlyvist (Meat and Justice) This outdoor restaurant has a little playground next to it where children can play while you enjoy your grilled meat.

Bilka This cafe is spacious enough to comfortably wheel a stroller into. It has high chairs, two kids' tables, drawing supplies and a few toys, as well a children's menu.

Green café This vegan café/restaurant has a carpeted second floor with low tables surrounding an open "play area", where kids can roll around and play with toys from the toy basket. Shoes must be removed in this area.

Celentano This well-known Ukrainian pizzeria has a kid's playroom in the basement of its most popular Ploshcha Rynok location (on Halytska street).

Del Pesto Located near Ivan Franko University, this Italian restaurant has a very large kids' play area downstairs, a high chair, and kid friendly menu options.

Vapiano This modern Italian chain restaurant in the Rius hotel is child-friendly with children's seats available and a small children's corner complete with a chalkboard. It has an open kitchen and works on a smart card system.

La famiglia This purpose built modern family restaurant offers a casual and relaxing atmosphere in which to enjoy a family meal. However it is located outside the centre in the Sykhiv district so it is best to take a taxi there.

Cooking classes

Some restaurants offer cooking classes for kids, usually on Sundays. Here are the names of a few of them, who have offered cooking classes in the past: Sushiya, Green Café, and Miaso i spravedlyvist (Meat and Justice). Call or check their web sites for upcoming classes.

KYIV
KYIV HOTELS

Kyiv also has a large selection of modern hotels to choose from, and short-term apartment rentals are also popular.

Kyiv's recommended upscale international luxury chain hotels include the **Hyatt Regency**, the **Hilton Kyiv**, the **Radisson Blu** and **InterContinental**. For a more boutique experience the new **11 Mirrors Design Hotel** and **Opera Hotel** feature highly. More reasonably priced hotels include the **Khreshchatyk Hotel**, **Hotel Ukraine** overlooking the Maidan, **the Ibis Kiev Shevchenko Boulevard**, and the **Kozatskiy** hotel next to the Maidan.

Worth a mention is the relatively new **Park Hotel Golosievo**. A few metro stops away from the city centre, its unique location in Holosiivkyi Park is great for those who want a break from city centre action, or for young families.

KYIV ATTRACTIONS

Being a large city with a long and rich history, there are many attractions to visit in Kyiv; in fact, more than can fit in what is meant to be a brief overview. As in the Lviv section, I have provided a list of options and links to help you plan your time there.

As mentioned, Kyiv has an efficient metro system, which is very cheap and makes the city easy to navigate. Some of the metro stations in the city centre are the deepest in the world, doubling up as bomb shelters in the Cold War, so be prepared for a long escalator ride. You can find a map here: *http://subway.umka.org/map-kiev.html*

Independent Walking Tour Depending on where you are staying, you might find some interesting corners to explore in your neighbourhood. To wander around the centre, your best bet is to get on the metro and head to Maidan Nezalezhnosti or Khreschatyk station to get right to the centre, or to Zoloti Vorota to see the Golden Gates or exit at the Poshtova Ploshcha stop to wander around the Podil "old town". **Here are some spots you might want to check out on your own:**

Maidan Nezalezhnosti Located along the Khreshchatyk central boulevard, this centralsquare has existed since before the 10th century with different appearances and names. The name means Independence Square and is often referred to simply as *"Maidan"*. It has been the main site of two revolutions in the past in the past 12 years. The current site was redesigned in 2001.

Golden Gates This museum is a reconstruction of the famous main entrance to the capital city of 11th century Kyivan Rus. The current representation was built in 1982 and next to it is a monument to Kyivan Rus Grand Prince Yaroslav the Wise.

Andriivskyi Uzviz This is a windy street that also connects upper downtown Kyiv with the lower Podil area. It gets its name from St Andrew's Church, which is located halfway down the street. On the weekends there is a popular arts market where art, handicrafts, folk wares and souvenirs are sold.

Kyiv Funicular After exploring the Andriivskyi Uzviz on foot, you can make your return trip in the Kyiv funicular, which also connects upper and lower Kyiv. Built in 1902-1905, it is an entertaining ride with a great view. The journey is only 3 minutes one-way and costs 3 UAH (about 12 cents US). The funicular is still used by Kyivites as  a mode of transportation, but mainly it's used as a scenic attraction.

Sculpture Alley Originally built in 1980 but with new additions since 2009, this alleyway of sculptures is a unique and artistically inspiring place to go for a short walk.

Golden Domed Churches

St. Sophia's Cathedral This magnificent cathedral and adjoining museum dates back to the times of Kyivan Rus. It was named one of the Seven Wonders of

Ukraine in a 2007 Ukraine-wide contest. It is an Eastern Orthodox Church but regular services are not held there due to controversy surrounding which specific branch of the church it should belong to.

St. Michael's Golden-Domed Monastery This breath-taking monastery is located just opposite the St. Sophia Cathedral and is a fully functioning religious institution. Originally built in 1108-1113, it was destroyed first during a Tatar invasion and then during Soviet times but was rebuilt in 1997-1999 after Ukraine regained independence.

St. Andrew's Church or Andriivskyi Church Built in the years 1747 to 1754 by Italian architect Francesco Bartolomeo Rastrelli in Baroque style, this Orthodox Church now holds regular mass, after lengthy periods of closure due to political reasons or renovation. Legend has it that Andrew the Apostle, one of the twelve apostles, travelled through present day Ukraine along the Dnipro river, and erected a cross on the spot where St Andrew's church now stands. According to the legend, he predicted that a great Christian city would be built there.

Pecherska Lavra Caves Monastery Many tourists, both

local and international, seem to be drawn to this monastery complex due to its ornate architecture and ancient history. You must pay to enter and you have the option of exploring the burial caves, which includes walking down narrow, dark corridors to see the coffins where the Church's saints are buried. You can also buy tickets for a 3-hour English language tour. Women should make sure to wear a headscarf and modest clothing.

Guided Walking Tours

If you'd like to try a walking tour with an English-speaking guide, below are links to some companies who offer this. *http://www.kievtours.com/ http://www.activeukraine.com/contact-us/*

Culinary Tour

If you have time and are interested in cooking, Active Ukraine also offers culinary tours.

Pyrohiv National Museum of Ukrainian Architecture and Culture Pyrohiv, or Pyrogovo as it is commonly called, is an open-air museum featuring traditional Ukrainian rural architecture, including clay huts and wooden churches, and objects traditionally used in daily life. A trip out to Pyrohiv on a local mini bus is an enjoyable way of spending the day outdoors and learning more about Ukraine's past. The museum hosts many traditional Ukrainian holidays and festivals year round. *http://pyrohiv.com.ua/en/*

Kyiv Bus tour If you prefer touring the city in the comfort of a bus, the company Open Kiev offers daily tours lasting 1 hour and 30 minutes, which stop at major sites including the Pecherska Lavra, the "Motherland" statue, Bessarabskyi market, the Golden Gate, the main churches, and more.

Tours are offered in Ukrainian, Russian, English, German, Italian, and Spanish. *http://openkiev.com.ua/en/tours/bus/*

Dynamo Kyiv Football Match Being a club with a legendary history, it is worth catching a big derby game with Shakhtar Donetsk or a Champions League match involving another top European club if you get the chance. Dynamo Kyiv play in the recently rebuilt Olympic Stadium with a 70,000 capacity, located in the very centre of town.

KYIV ARTS AND CULTURE

Kyiv Opera Theatre

There are a multitude of arts and cultural excursions to indulge in every day of the year in Kyiv, with a large number of theatres, museums, galleries and other cultural venues.

KYIV THEATRES

Any trip to Kyiv should include at least one night out to view a performance at one of the many beautiful theatres. The Tripadvisor website currently lists 53 theatres in the capital city. Below are a few of them.

National Opera of Ukraine Like the Lviv Opera House, the Kyiv Opera House is stunning and offers shows featuring experienced performers who present delightful renditions of internationally renowned and traditional Ukrainian operas and ballets. Many tourists are impressed by the world-class performances, beautiful costumes, lovely architecture and fantastic orchestra. *http://www.opera.com.ua/en/*

Operetta The Kyiv Operetta offers a range of performances, including vocal and instrumental music, dance, ballet and elements of pop art, including such shows as the ballet *Carmen*, the "musical story" *Snow White*, and the musicals *"Welcome to Ukraine"* and even *The Sound of Music*. *http://operetta.com.ua/?lang=en*

Les Kurbas Theatre Just like the Lviv Les Kurbas theatre, this venue features experimental plays using new methods and approaches. It has a repertoire of about 60 shows. *http://www.kurbas.org.ua/en/centre.html*

National Philharmonic of Ukraine The Philharmotic offers a large variety of performances including chamber music, classic symphonies, folk music or more popular modern concerts. The acoustics are very good. *http://www.filarmonia.com.ua/en*

National Ivan Franko Academic Theatre This is one of the most popular and well-known theatres in Kyiv, located in a beautiful building near the government quarter. It shows classic Ukrainian and international plays and many written by popular young Ukrainian writers. It has featured many prominent Ukrainian actors. *http://ft.org.ua/*

Kyiv Art Galleries

PinchukArtCentre ThePinchukArt Centre is a modern art gallery opened in 2006 by Ukrainian businessman Viktor Pinchuk and, according to its website, is an "international centre for contemporary art of the 21st century... and an open platform for artists", where the works of many prominent Ukrainian and international artists are featured. Admission is free and the gallery is open daily (except Mondays) from 12-9pm. The Pinchuk Art Centre has four floors of exhibits and a video lounge and café on the top floor. *http://pinchukartcentre.org/en/*

AVS Art This gallery features prominent artists from all over Ukraine. Their goal is to maintain a high level of art in Ukraine. According to their site, they are always happy to welcome visitors, art collectors and artists. *http://avsart.com.ua/*

Triptych Art The Triptych art gallery, centrally located near the top of Andriyivskyi uzviz, prides itself on the professionalism of the artists it features and its international art contacts. *http://www.triptych-art.com/*

Bottega Art Gallery This is a small art gallery specialising in exhibits of modern art (including paintings, sculptures, and photography) of both experienced artists and young artists just starting out. They are affiliated with the next-door **Shcherbenko Art Centre** *http://shcherbenkoartcentre.com/en/*

Museums

Out of the many museums in Kyiv, here is a short list to get your started.

National Museum of Folk Decorative Arts Though this museum has a bit of a Soviet feel, it houses an impressive amount of displays of beautiful folk arts, carpets and embroidered clothes, sculptures and paintings. It often hosts special exhibits of famous Ukrainian artists. *http://www.mundm.kiev.ua/*

Ivan Honchar museum The original collection of Ukrainian artifacts at this museum was gathered by Ivan Honchar in his travels around Ukraine. It includes embroidered clothes, pottery, Easter eggs, folk instruments, amateur paintings and more. The artifacts were kept in his apartment until the museum was established in 1993. The museum now features 15,000 artifacts from the 16th to 20th centuries. Special events programs for children such as folk song workshops or making traditional Ukrainian dishes. *http://honchar.org.ua/*

Literary Memorial Museum of Mikhail Bulgakov This museum/memorial house is the former home of Mikhail Bulgakov and is featured in his novel *The White Guard*. The museum includes 300 of Bulgakov's personal items and reflects the life of the famous writer. *http://bulgakov.org.ua/*

Kyiv Museum of Wax Figures If you're looking for an amusing outing, head to the Museum of Wax Figures. It features a host of well known historical, political, literary and athletic figures, as well as those from music and show business. *http://www.wax.com.ua/*

Chornobyl Musuem This museum was set up to document the 1986 tragic nuclear explosion at the Chornobyl Power station, located 134 km outside of Kyiv. The museum itself is isn't as well designed or interactive as it could be, but does offer some interesting information and over 7000 exhibits. *http://chornobylmuseum.kiev.ua/en/*

Bohdan and Varvara Khanenko Museum / Kyiv Museum of Western and Oriental Art Considered one of the top three museums of Western art in Ukraine, this museum was built by private art collectors Bohdan and Varvara Khanenko. It survived both wars, though over 300,000 artifacts of the original collection were taken from the museum, some sold by the Soviet government and others stolen by the Nazis. Though not huge in size, this cosy museum hosts a large collection of European and Eastern Art (from Japan, China, Iran, and Turkey), including unique Byzantine icons of the 6-7th centuries, and works by Rembrandt, Donatello, Velasquez and Durer. Be sure to check the opening hours before heading to the museum.

Yanukovych's Mezhyhirya Mansion a.k.a "Museum of Corruption" If you want to see the scale of corruption and misuse of power of former escapee president Viktor Yanukovych, you can take a trip to his abandoned mansion, which has been turned into a museum open to the public. You can take a local bus from the Heroiv Dnipro metro stop, or arrange a taxi and a private tour in English at much higher price.

KYIV RESTAURANTS

Kyiv has many options for restaurants and new ones are popping up all the time. I'll keep my recommendations to a minimum tried and true short list. The prices at many of Kyiv's restaurants are higher than in Lviv.

Pizzeria Napule This was one of my favourite restaurants when I was living in Kyiv and I see it still makes top ten lists today. The authentic Italian food, complete with delicious wood-oven pizza, salads with fresh Italian cheeses, and delicate desserts, is simply mouth-watering.

Osteria Pantagruel offers a classic, formal Italian dining experience in the centre of Kyiv and has a nice selection of tasty dishes including grilled vegetables, risottos, a pesto carpaccio, and a rabbit casserole. The wine selection is excellent.

Shoti is currently one of the most popular Georgian restaurants in Kyiv. Trying Georgian food is a must-do while in Ukraine. My favourites include the Badrijani eggplant rolls topped with pomegranate seeds, the warm bean dishes, the traditional Georgian shashlyk (shish kabob) meats and the "khachapuri", pizza type breads oozing with cheese.

Pervak This is a delightful charming turn of the 20th century themed restaurant near Ploshcha Lva Tostoho metro. The food is Ukrainian/traditional Central European of a high standard. The service is excellent and caters for western visitors without feeling touristy. This established restaurant will always guarantee an enjoyable evening out.

Citronelle A more modern twist on the Mediterranean theme, Citronelle is a relaxed and pleasant restaurant with a good range of dishes at reasonable process. Its location near the Opera House makes for a convenient dining spot.

Tike This clean and modern restaurant in Podil is good for grills and Turkish cuisine.

Puzata Khata This cafeteria-style eatery deserves a mention since it has been popular for years among tourists and locals alike and known as the best place to get a quick home-style meal in many locations around the country. Choose from a selection of salads, meat dishes, and side dishes. They also offer breakfasts and sweet dishes such as crèpes filled with apples or cottage cheese.

Sushiya No listing of restaurants in Kyiv would be complete without mention of a sushi restaurant. This chain offers good value and consistent quality.

Kyiv TAKE OUT

Ordering take-out is quite popular in Kyiv if you are not bothered by the lengthy wait times during peak hours (usually an hour to an hour and a half). The following site offers take-out options from restaurants all over the city: *http://ekipazh-service.com.ua/*

KYIV CAFES

Kyivites enjoy their coffee, but with the quicker pace of work they don't seem to have as much time for coffee breaks as in Lviv. That said, there are still plenty of modern cafes and your best bet is to try out a few cafés close to wherever you're staying. From my experience, you can get a decent cappuccino at most nice restaurants or cafés but I tend to avoid some of the chain cafés whose cakes and sandwiches don't look homemade.

Wolkonsky This is a French style café and bakery located in the Premier Palace hotel, with other locations around Kyiv. Besides their tasty pastries, the menu has a good selection of soups, salads, sandwiches and desserts and includes sides such as hummus, babaganoush and quinoa. It also has a children's play area (with a babysitter onsite on weekends) making it a nice weekend morning family café outing.

Lviv Chocolate Workshop also has locations in Kyiv, where it feels much less touristy. As in Lviv, kids and adults can sign up for chocolate making classes.

Repriza is a café and bakery with four locations in Kyiv, offering hot croissants and other pastries, breakfasts and a selection of light meals.

ACTIVITIES FOR KIDS IN KYIV

Parks

Shevchenko Park is a very popular spot for families raising children in the city centre area, though it is smaller than other parks. There is a playground with a sand pit, and on the weekends, for a small fee children can have a pony ride or take a spin in a toy car. *http://www.lifeinkiev.com/taras-shevchenko-park/*

Holosiivskyi Park Located in a pleasant suburb 15 minutes from the centre, Holosiivksky Park is a great place to go for a family walk, cycle ride, or a game of Frisbee or ball. There are several playgrounds with sand pits and it also has a couple of areas with amusement park rides for children.

Shopping malls, skating rinks, bowling alleys and cinemas are very popular in Kyiv and you will be able to find many throughout the city. I would suggest starting by doing a quick search in Google (either in English or using an online translator) to find the location nearest you.

It is common for families to take out a membership with a fitness centre that has a pool, a gym and group classes for adults and children. Some have children's play rooms where kids can be supervised while their parents are working out.

Kyiv Skating Rinks
http://relax.ua/sport/ice-skating-rinks/lang/ua

Swimming pools and water parks

In addition to the pools in fitness clubs, some of the older public pools can also be a good option. The following link has a list of public pools. *http://www.swimming-pool.vitava.com.ua/*

City Beach Club in Ocean Plaza Mall This beach club with two large outdoor swimming pools is located on the roof of the popular Ocean Plaza shopping mall near the Lybidska metro station. *http://www.oceanplaza.com.ua/en/entertainments/tc/citybeachclub*

Dream Island Water park The Obolon district has a large shopping centre with an indoor water park for weekend or evening fun. *http://aqua.dreamtown.ua/*

Aqua Park in Brovary This water park has pools, a Jacuzzi, water slides, a wave pool, saunas, and a restaurant. The roof retracts in the summer months. It's definitely worth it to make the 25km drive from Kyiv city centre (about 30 min without traffic). *http://aquapark-terminal.com.ua/*

Indoor Play Centre

Kidlandia Though a bit of a drive from the city centre, your kids can have fun at Kidlandia, which is a children's "country", where they can try their hand at various adult jobs such as playing doctor, working as a cashier in a supermarket, riding in a fire brigade car, or in a radio studio. All of the work areas are very realistic and kids are sure to enjoy their time there. *http://kidlandia.ua/ua*

Kyiv Children's Theatres

Kyiv Academic Puppet Theatre This is a beautiful, newly renovated children's theatre but adults might also enjoy a visit, either to attend a show or just admire the architecture. There is also a small doll museum inside which can be visited for free. *http://www.akadempuppet.kiev.ua/*

Kyiv Lypky Theatre Originally founded as a youth theatre, this theatre now offers shows for both adults and children. Check their site for a list of upcoming shows. *http://tuz.kiev.ua/*

Kyiv Children's Opera and Ballet Theatre This theatre offers operas and ballets geared towards children, such as *Snow White*, *The Nutcracker*, and *Adventures of Huckleberry Fin*, among others. *http://www.musictheatre.kiev.ua/*

Other Activities

Experimentarium This is a children's museum with a permanent exhibition of interactive stations with mechanics, electromagnetism, acoustics and optics, anatomy and more. *http://www.experimentanium.com.ua/*

Natural History Museum This large museum has many interesting displays (zoology, geology, palaeontology and more), which can be enjoyed by both adults and children, though some are a bit Soviet looking.

Ivan Honchar museum As mentioned above, this museum often has folk arts workshops and programs for kids.

Kyiv Zoo A trip to the Kyiv Zoo can be a fun family day out. Though it's about 20 minutes from the city centre by car or about a 30 minute metro ride to the stop Politekhnichnyi Instytut, I'm sure young children will agree that its worth the journey. *http://zoo.kiev.ua/*

KYIV CAFES AND RESTAURANTS WITH PLAY AREAS

Going to a restaurant or café is a very popular family weekend activity in Kyiv. Several restaurants have areas for kids to play, or drawing supplies and high chairs on hand.

Wolkonsky As mentioned in the Kyiv café section, Wolkonsky café has a large children's play area and on weekends there is often a nanny on site to watch the kids.   *http://wolkonsky.com/ua*

Home Café Located in Holosiivkyi district, this cozy café offers great food and a nice children's activity corner with puzzles and toys. *http://www.homecafe.com.ua/#1*

Glossary Organic Café Located near the Zoloti Vorota metro station, this café has a tasty natural menu and a kid's table with toys and drawing accessories. *http://glossary.ua/#/en/*

Korchma Taras Bulba Restaurant. This traditional Ukrainian restaurant has a great area for kids to play and is welcoming to families with young children. *http://tarasbulba.kiev.ua/*

Dvor Holosiivskyi Located in Holosiivsky Park, this restaurant is a great place to stop in after some family fun in the park. It has an outdoor playground for children and specializes in food from the Caucasus. *http://dvorgoloseevskiy.com.ua/ru/*

Pryroda (Nature) Family Restaurant and Park Located in the Dniprovsky district, this amazing park complex has been specially designed for families. One whole floor has been dedicated to an "edutainment" kids section, where kids can do Science experiments and other educational activities. *http://ilovepriroda.com/*

Outside Kyiv, there are also a few great family restaurants, including:

Rozhulyayevo Grill Restaurant This outdoor restaurant has extensive grounds and an indoor kids play centre. The play centre offers weekend art classes and summer camps. *http://razgulyaevo.com.ua/*

Chumatskyi Shliakh This restaurant-hotel has a mini zoo, making it an entertaining and educational.

Podkova is a beautiful restaurant-hotel complex that specializes in hosting banquets and special events and family lunches or dinners. The outdoor pool and sandbox are great for summer months. *http://www.podkova-restoran.com.ua/en/*

Kids' restaurants

Baby Bar specializes in children's birthday parties and offers a child-friendly menu. If there is no scheduled birthday, you can also stop in for a coffee and a meal while your children play in the playroom. *http://baby-bar.kiev.ua/*

Baby Rock Café is a children's café also used mainly for hosting trendy and extravagant birthday parties. There is an adult-friendly restaurant next door called Gastro rock, where parents can enjoy each other's company in a quieter venue while their children party. *http://www.babyrock.com.ua*

PART III – PRACTICAL ADVICE AND INSIGHTS

ARRIVING IN UKRAINE

Depending on where you are coming from and how much experience you have in global travel, arriving in Ukraine may bring on a fair bit of culture shock. For me, despite having spent many years in Ukraine, I still seem to get culture shock for the first day or two each time I arrive, particularly if I am flying through or from clean and organized Germany. Thankfully, proceeding through the modern airports in Kyiv and Lviv themselves are usually smooth experiences, particularly in the newly built Lviv airport, which deals with a relatively small number of planes and passengers.

The first sign that you are in Ukraine (after you have hopefully cleared passport control and picked up your bags with no issues), can be the rather annoying appearance of pushy taxi drivers. You can avoid them by having someone meet you at the airport if possible or by hurrying past them and heading to an official airport taxi service desk. They will provide you with a rate up front (currently 120 UAH/ 5 USD in Lviv) and the assigned driver will help you take your things to the car. Kyiv airport has a fleet of official taxis called Sky Taxi, which you can check out here: *https://kbp.aero/en/about/press-center/news/2013/404/*

If arriving to Lviv by train, perhaps the night train from Krakow or Budapest, it's safe and easy to take public transport to wherever you need to go. You can catch the local tram into the city centre, which is just a handful of stops away. In Kyiv, on the other hand, the central train station is usually very busy and the metro stop located adjacent to the train station is usually very crowded. But taking the metro to the city centre is an inexpensive and quick option.

As you travel through the city your visual perception will quickly be hit with many contrasting images, both ancient and modern, beautiful and ugly, and you will get your first glimpse of all of the contrasts that can be seen in Ukraine; Soviet era Lada cars driving next to BMWs, large new high-end western brand stores next to grimy looking kiosks, big swanky restaurants on some streets and grannies selling their garden or farm produce out of plastic bags on others.

Alongside the many positive aspects of living in Ukraine come some of the downsides. One is that the cities feel somewhat dirtier than in other parts of Europe, with streets being cleaned less frequently, and recycling/waste management programmes (including the responsible disposal of various items or proper exhaust filters on cars) not having fully taken off. However, once you are in your comfort zone you can figure out how to work around these inconveniences, such as knowing where the closest available place to wash your hands is. When in Ukraine it is wise to make hand washing a more frequent habit.

That said, many places in Ukraine feel magical once you have had a chance to settle in and explore, and any initial culture shock will usually fade into excitement or endearment for the many charms and surprises you will soon discover.

FINDING A PLACE TO STAY

From my experience, finding a place to stay for a few days, a few weeks, months, or years, is much easier than in any other place I've lived. Besides hotels, many apartments are specially marketed to foreigners or visitors from other parts of Ukraine and are available for short or long stays. Most can be booked online in advance on English websites. For longer stays, you can sometimes negotiate a price with the landlord, and if your situation changes you can usually amend your agreement or contract.

Through Airbnb you can find many well-appointed apartments in Lviv and Kyiv from which to choose. However, we preferred finding places managed by owners and not companies. The renovated apartments available are specifically marketed to foreigners or wealthier tourists from the capital and thus the prices are much higher. If you're not picky about the amenities where you are staying, it is possible to find very cheap accommodation in basic apartments or in hostels. If you want to try to look at what apartments are available for locals at local rates, you can try a search in Ukrainian by entering "оренда квартир у києві" or "оренда квартир у Львові" (which translates to apartment rental in Kyiv/Lviv).

If you are looking for something longer term and at a lower price, the general practice, as in many cities in the world, is to use an agent to whom you pay a commission (usually a month's rent) if they find you a place. From my experience, there are many decent apartments available, but for long-term stays it does take a while to find a place that would meet all your criteria. Make sure to specify if you need access to running water all day long, decent heaters for winter months, or a lift. In Kyiv, many apartment buildings have a "concierge", really a fancy term for a granny who checks who is coming and going into the building, which can be reassuring. Some places have actual security guards. In the centre of Lviv, there are not many lifts, so if you will need one, make sure to look for a first floor apartment or stay in a hotel.

We have stayed in a few areas around the centre of Lviv and have determined that for us the *Ploshcha rynok* pedestrian zone is the best place to be, particularly with kids. The streets are safe for walking, and due to the lack of cars it is pleasant to keep your windows open on warm days. The only downside can be noise in the evenings, though there are some quieter streets.

Which area of the city is best to find an apartment in? This depends on your budget and how much you are willing to use public transport. Generally in Ukrainian cities it is best for expats to live in city centres, though the prices are much higher. Another popular option is to live in a quieter area by a park from which you can easily reach the centre by public transportation.

BUYING ESSENTIALS

Ukrainian cities are full of shops and kiosks selling a wide variety of products. Unlike some European or North American cities I have been to, shops stay open quite late and there are always some nearby shops open 24 hours in case you need to urgently buy some essentials. There are 24 hour pharmacies, some of which even offer free delivery to your home (often if you spend a minimum amount), anything from water to paracetamol, to cough drops to emergency diapers (which, incidentally, can be bought as single items in many pharmacies). Most of the products you might need can be found either at your nearby supermarket, *produkty* shop, cosmetics shop or pharmacy.

On the next page are the Ukrainian words for some essential items you might need. If you aren't fluent in Ukrainian, pronouncing them as clearly and confidently as possible and pointing at what you need should get you what you want.

Vocabulary of essential items

Coffee	Кава	Kava
Tea	Чай	Chai
Water	Вода	Voda
Yoghurt	Йогурт	Yogurt
Cheese	Сир	Syr

Milk	Молоко	Moloko
Butter	Масло	Maslo
Bananas	Банани	Banany
Apples	Яблука	Yabluka
Bread	Хліб	Khlib / Hlib
Beer	Пиво	Pyvo
Wine	Вино	Vyno
Ticket	Квиток	Kvytok
Pharmacy	Аптека	Apteka
Shampoo	Шампунь	Shampun
Soap	Мило	Mylo
Diapers/Nappies	Памперси	Pampersy
Feminine pads	Прокладки	Prokladky
Toilet paper	Туалетний папір	Tualetnyi papir

"the "y" is pronounced like a short I, as in "it" or "win"

Pharmacies

Below are links to websites for some well-known pharmacies (*aptekas*) that deliver. Unfortunately whether or not you will be able to make your order in English will depend on the language skills of whoever answers the phone.

LVIV

DS Phramacy This pharmacy has an English language website where you can see their products and a list of locations. It doesn't offer delivery, but they are open until 9pm, Monday through Saturday and until 8pm on Sundays. *http://www.ds.lviv.ua/en*

KYIV AND LVIV

Simeyna apteka This pharmacy offers delivery services between 8am and 9pm daily and free delivery for orders over 100 UAH (about 5 USD). *http://sa.lviv.ua/*

KYIV

E-apteka This pharmacy offers 24-hour delivery. Delivery rates vary so you will need to ask when you make your order. *http://e-apteka.com.ua/*

Apteka dobroho dnya

This pharmacy offers delivery services between 8am and 9pm on weekdays, and 9am and 6pm on weekends. Delivery is free on orders of more than 100 UAH. *https://www.add.ua/*

Apteka 911

This pharmacy offers delivery services between 8am and 9pm daily. Be aware that in order to qualify for delivery services, your items must total at least 350 UAH (about $18).   *http://apteka911.com.ua/*

COOKING FOR YOURSELF & SHOPPING FOR FOOD

Bazaars /markets

We relish the experience of going to Ukrainian open air markets in the summer months. There is something about the look and smell of the vegetables and fruit, most of which have been home grown in nearby villages, which is so appealing to the senses. We love coming home with bags full of colourful sweet smelling vegetables, which inspire us to cook seasonal dishes, and often make fresh salads or soups. Although they aren't certified as organic, the rich Ukrainian soil and the low use of pesticides by small time/private farmers result in the most natural tasting produce without an organic label you can find. Don't assume all the vegetables you see in the market are organic though; your best bet is to buy from grannies as they usually sell produce from their own backyard gardens. Also look for *domashniy* dairy products from certified shops, like "Cheese Voyage", listed below. The word "domashniy" in Ukrainian is used to refer to natural, home grown food. It's like the Ukrainian equivalent of organic.

Cheese Voyage / Syrni mandry in Lviv This tucked away artisanal/ "organic" cheese shop offers a variety of artisanal cheeses, yoghurt, sausage, home made pesto, granola bars, bread and more. A must try if you are near the Halytskyi bazaar in Lviv or near the other locations listed on their website. *https://www.facebook.com/Cheesevoyage?fref=ts*

Supermarkets and *Produkty* shops

Supermarkets didn't always exist in Ukraine but now they are just as common and popular here in Ukrainian cities as you would expect in any large city you visit. The range and quality of goods is impressive, though you might have to use a dictionary to make sure you understand the labels.

In the small *produkty* (ПРОДУКТИ / ПРОДУКТОВИЙ МАГАЗИН) shops you have to ask a lady behind a counter to hand you each item you need as she adds it up on a calculator, or in some cases, an abacus (!). There are still a lot of them across the country, so in some cases a *produkty* shop will be your closest option to buy snacks or water. Remember, you will need to know how to say "Дайте ___ будь ласка" which translates as "Give me _____ please".

Lviv Supermarkets

Arsen The city centre mini-mall "Roksolana" has a small but convenient supermarket in the basement. *http://www.roksolana.ua/en/market/*

Opera Market in Opera Passage This city centre mini-mall also has a small supermarket on it's -1 floor offering high range and specialty items, along with standard Ukrainian goods. *http://www.operapassage.com/en*

Silpo at Forum Mall is an impressive and large supermarket offering an extensive variety of Ukrainian and imported products. It also has a café, a restaurant, and a deli where you can order a variety of prepared

salads, meat dishes and other Ukrainian favourites.
http://lviv.multi.eu/stores/silpo/?portfolioID=28

Kyiv Supermarkets

Megamarket Kyiv's large central supermarket is popular among expats and locals alike and offers an extensive selection of everything you would expect to find in a supermarket, including a selection of imported goods. The city centre location also has a bakery and a fresh juice stand in it. Megamarket also offers online shopping and delivery. *http://megamarket.ua/ua*

Silpo / Сільпо This is another major supermarket chain with an extensive array of goods, with an online shopping and delivery option.

Ashan/АШАН The French supermarket "Auchan" opened its first "hypermarket" in Ukraine in 2008. There is a large Ashan in the central "Ocean Plaza" shopping mall near the Lybidska metro station. *http://www.auchan.ua/uk/shops/auchan-libidska/*

"Le Silpo" in Mandarin plaza is a more gourmet version of the regular Silpo and is a popular supermarket for those living in the centre closer to Bessarabskyi market. Prices are higher than in most supermarkets. They offer some delicacies and specialty items. *http://mandarinplaza.ua/ru/brendy/36-eda/88-lesilpo.html*

Shop online and have your groceries delivered

Online grocery delivery services are increasingly popular in Ukraine. You can try the following sites:

Iz sela This online shop promises natural foods "from the village/farm" for a slightly higher price. Delivery is 40 UAH or free on orders over 500 UAH. In order to qualify for delivery, you must spend at least 120 UAH. If in doubt, don't be afraid to question where a particular food has come from. *http://lviv.izsela.com.ua/*

Hit 24 This online supermarket has an extensive selection of everything you might find in a regular supermarket. Delivery is 30 UAH. *http://hit24.lviv.ua/ua/?start*

Megamarket as described above   *http://megamarket.ua/ua*

Furshet This is a good Kyiv supermarket chain and it offers delivery services. *http://efurshet.com/*

Silpo as described above.

Buying Organic In Ukraine

There are now many Ukrainian companies with organic labels, which also offer gluten-free baked goods, though Ukrainians don't always trust that these companies are completely "certified". You might be able to find organic products in regular supermarkets. Here are some specialty organic shops to check out.

LVIV

Eco cosmetics - *http://www.eco.lviv.ua-*
Green market - *http://green-market.com.ua/*

KYIV, with delivery to other cities

Eco-club - *http://ecoclub.ua/*
Eco Lavka - *http://eco-lavca.ua/*
Natur Boutique - *http://natur-boutique.ua/*

Bottled Water
It is not advised to drink tap water in Ukraine unless your sink has an additional filter (a separate, smaller tap). Many Ukrainians boil tap water for their tea or when cooking, as I did when I first lived in Kyiv, but I would advise sticking to bottled water. Tests have show the tap water in Lviv to be quite clean, but many city pipes are old and rusty so without a filter the water can look slightly rusty in colour. Please note that it is good practice to ask at restaurants if their food has been prepared using tap water or bottled water.

The "Morshynska" brand, which comes from the

Carpathian mountain region, has a very good reputation. If you are renting an apartment for a short stay, bottled water is not usually provided, and you may find yourself making frequent trips to your nearest supermarket or *produkty* shop to purchase bottled water. You can buy easy-to-carry 6 litre water bottles. If you are staying longer in Ukraine, it is worth organizing a weekly water delivery, costing about 40-50 UAH (about 2USD) per 19 litre bottle, plus an initial deposit for the bottles.

Alaska is a branch of the Morshynska company. *http://alaska.ua/uk/*

Clearwater has an English website for orders in Kyiv. *http://www.clearwater.ua/en/delivery*

GETTING AROUND

To me, minimizing time needed to get around Ukrainian cities makes a huge difference in terms of the overall experience of your stay. As a person who loves to be able to walk or cycle wherever I need to go, I appreciate that this is possible in Lviv. I was also pleased that in Kyiv I never felt I needed a car until I experienced raising a small child there. Many foreigners who live in Ukraine long term choose to buy cars and obtain a Ukrainian driver's licence or use their international one.

Trams In Lviv, the most convenient mode of public transportation is probably the trams, though they do break down on occasion. Kyiv has 23 tram routes.

Marshrutkas During peak hours, Ukrainian mini buses (*marshrutkas*) can be crowded, with drivers not always adhering to safety standards, and a risk of being pickpocketed. I have never experienced this but several Ukrainian friends have. Sometimes, though, *marshrutkas* might be your best or only option. Be aware that it is a common practice to get on the mini bus at either door and pass your bus fare to the person in front of you, until it gets passed to the driver. Don't be surprised if someone hands you money on a bus – just pass it along to the person in front of you.

Metro The Kyiv metro is usually a hassle-free, safe and quick mode of transport, though it can get very crowded during peak hours. See the Kyiv section for a link to the metro map.

Taxis/Drivers On the plus side, taxis (and personal

drivers) are pretty affordable, but you can't always be guaranteed that they will have working seatbelts or won't smell heavily of cigarette smoke.

Here are my **tips for getting around**:

1) For longer distances, do not travel on *marshrutkas*. The swerving can feel stressful enough, and if they are jam packed with people it will also be very uncomfortable.

2) Do not stray from major urban areas unless you are in a taxi or being driven by a friend. In Lviv, this means stick around the centre or in your comfort zone unless you have a lot of time on your hands and are in a very laid back mood. Going to an unfamiliar location on public transportation can be very frustrating and tiresome.

3) If you are looking for a cheap cab ride, you can usually flag an unmarked car down on the street by gently waving your lowered hand (with palm facing downwards) or you can call up any taxi service. If you would like a cleaner car with functioning seatbelts, look up "VIP taxi services". With children this is an absolute must.

FINDING WHAT YOU NEED

Though the Internet is a great source for finding what you need in most cities, English language sites in Ukraine may be limited. Thankfully, many web browsers these days offer automatic translations.

Much information in Ukraine is still found out through word of mouth, be it directions to an unknown location or recommendations on a variety of services. Perhaps this stems from a Soviet collectivist past or a lack of efficient information sharing systems. Ukrainians are not shy about approaching people to ask for assistance and you shouldn't be either. Most will be very helpful and friendly.

You can also try to the tourist information centres listed above.

As in the West, online shopping has become increasingly popular, and most of what you might need can be bought online, though navigating Ukrainian language sites might be a challenge. There is also a new private "alternative" postal service called Nova Poshta that you may use for deliveries at one of their many pick up points located in main cities.

Here are links to some online shops that might be useful:

Foxtrot electronics *http://www.foxtrot.com.ua/*

Ikea delivery shop in Lviv (imported from Poland): *https://ikea-club.com.ua/ua/*

Ikea delivery in other cities *http://ua.ikeaukraine.com/*

Clothing for men, women and children
http://ua.nextdirect.com/en/

Nova Poshta private postal service *https://novaposhta.ua/*

Mobile Telephones

You might also need to buy a Ukrainian phone card for the duration of your stay. Most phone cards are inexpensive at around 20-30 UAH and can be purchased at a kiosk or mobile phone shop. You do not need to show your passport or sign a contract for pay-as-you go cards. The main mobile phone companies are Kyivstar, MTC, Life and Djuice. Sending text messages internationally is very affordable, but making international calls can be expensive, so it is best to call on Skype or Viber using the Internet connection in the place you are staying or at a café.

SAFETY

Thankfully, I have never had any safety issues while in Ukraine, probably because I take sensible precautions and don't go to unfamiliar places by myself, particularly at night. But higher crime rates, lower safety standards, and less reliable police services mean that you might need to be more cautious than you would be in your home country. The introduction of some reformed city police units since 2014 is a good effort to keep the streets safer. Please contact your embassy's websites for any current travel or safety warnings.

Driving hazards Be very careful when crossing streets and driving in Ukraine, as not all road users drive safely.

Late night safety Drunk individuals can be hazardous, particularly if they try to provoke a fight. Be aware that there have been instances of people being attacked on the streets late at night, including those attacked for having a different skin colour. Also, awareness of LGBT rights at the moment is poorly developed.

Homeless and beggars Be aware that some homeless individuals can become aggressive or refuse to go away unless you give them some money, but this is rare in my experience.

Scams Tourists are sometimes targeted for scams like the "wallet drop" or fraudulent bankcard use at ATMs.

Theft As mentioned, keep track of your valuables at all times, and leave any non necessary cards, ID docs and expensive items at home or locked in your hotel or apartment safe.

Bribery / corruption It is widely known that bribery and corruption are rampant in Ukraine, as this was one of the major reasons for both revolutions. It is very possible that you will not see any bribery when you are in Ukraine since it is often hidden from expats.

Random hooliganism /theft If you stay out late and go off the beaten path, you may see random acts of hooliganism and petty crime. A local friend recently saw three intoxicated young men trying to steal cobblestones at midnight from a municipal building site.

Hopefully you will not encounter any of the above possibilities. If you stay alert and aware and can get past the unpleasant aspects, you will truly enjoy yourself and your stay will be a great learning experience.

HEALTH CARE

You can rest assured that there are modern private medical facilities in many Ukrainian cities, including Lviv and Kyiv. I would particularly recommend American Medical Centres (AMC) in Kyiv or Lviv in case of medical emergencies, as their medical staff speak English and they adhere to American protocols. I had international health insurance through my employer and gave birth to my first daughter in a private clinic in Kyiv (ISIDA). It was an amazing 5 star experience. The facilities were impressive, with nightgowns, bathrobes, and toiletries provided. Recently, my youngest daughter needed a quick blood test in Lviv. I called the Medis Diagnostics centre and they sent a nurse over within an hour to take the blood sample. We had to pay an extra fee for home service and the nurse's taxi fare, but the rates were very reasonable.

We have also used the free Ukrainian national health care facilities and been quite happy with the results. If you stay in Ukraine long term you may find that family doctors who practice privately (ie they rent an office and accept payments for visits) are happy to offer advice over the phone at no extra cost, for example to determine the seriousness of an incident or interpret the results of a blood test. Also many doctors make house calls for an extra fee. Below are the names and addresses of medical facilities to keep at hand during your stay in Ukraine. One thing to be aware of is that Ukrainian doctors have been known to overexaggerate illnesses, so sometimes you might need to get a second opinion.

LVIV

AMC American Medical Center -
offers American standard healthcare, all doctors are English-speaking, direct billing with many international insurance companies *http://amcenters.com/en/*

Intersono -high level
of service for regular GP and pediatric appointments; some doctors may speak English; originally established as a fertility clinic and still offers those services. *http://intersono.ua/en/*

Medis Diagnostic centre -high level
of service for appointments with a variety of specialists; some doctors may speak English

KYIV

AMC American Medical Center(see the Lviv section above)

Borys -
provides "international" standard health care service and equipment, very reasonable rates (particularly if you need to pay out of pocket), Ukrainian speaking doctors, but some may speak English *http://www.boris.kiev.ua/*

Eurolab -
modern diagnostics lab, range of clinical services, 24 hour call centre, practices Evidence Based Medicine *http://clinic.eurolab.ua/*

CHILDCARE

Having lived in Ukraine with young children, I highly appreciate the child-care options I have available there compared to what I have experienced in North America. It is shocking for me to realise that while many American women cannot afford to stay at home with their new babies for more than a few weeks, Ukrainian women are legally guaranteed a 3-year maternity leave. They also have affordable child care options. In Ukraine, the first option is usually grandparents. Often after childbirth, the mother or daughter temporarily move in with the other for the first few weeks or months. In many cases, grandmothers take over all household and cooking tasks while new mothers catch up on lost sleep.

Nannies are common in Kyiv with the many career women there, and they are usually conscientious, responsible, and often help with housework. Having raised two children in Ukraine, I feel fortunate to have had the support of a few wonderful nannies and as a result never felt isolated or overburdened with all the responsibilities parenthood entails.

At the age of about three, and sometimes earlier, children can attend a state sponsored kindergarten which offers a hot lunch, outdoor play and small beds for nap time. The normal hours are 9am to 6pm. I can't guarantee that all kindergartens are of a high standard (in poorer areas many are lacking in modern equipment and toys), but there are many private or semi-private ones in Kyiv or Lviv which offer great programs and care.

BUSINESS

Some foreigners are attracted to the potential of Ukraine's large consumer market. If you are an experienced entrepreneur hoping to get into the Ukrainian market, it is best to contact the European Business Association (EBA) or the American Chamber of Commerce (AMCHAM) in Kyiv. Incidentally, Lviv seems to have become a new hub of the IT industry, with many skilled locals employed by foreign IT companies (and earning very high salaries). The garment industry is also developing, with companies such as Hugo Boss outsourcing many of their sewing needs to their Lviv partners.

ANECDOTES ON MEETING PEOPLE

From my experiences, Ukraine is one of the easiest countries to meet new people. You can usually always find a Ukrainian who will be interested in asking you about yourself, why you came to Ukraine, and what your life abroad is like. Recently, I tried out a particular yoga studio for the first time and was made to feel very welcome as soon as I got there, both by the instructor and by a few of the regulars, and there was quite a bit of chatter in the small change room. My six year old has a very easy time making friends, since in play areas other kids usually come up to her and say "Hi, my name is ___ and I am ___ years old. Let's play!" My daughter will smile and reply, and they will bounce off happily together. My daughters and I speak Ukrainian, but my husband has also had many experiences where people have gone out of their way to assist him, make him feel welcome, and use as much English as they could in the process.

You may also happen to meet people who are just happy to practice their English with a native speaker or any other non-native speaker who speaks English fluently. In the past this was especially exciting for Ukrainians as there wasn't much contact with people from Western countries or opportunities to travel abroad. For Ukrainians, fluency in another language is highly valued and many are eager to have real practice.

Some Ukrainians have gained their English fluency purely from books or formal school or university classes, and in that case you might notice them using archaic expressions or just funny sounding constructions. As a student in Lviv (at a time when the general level of English speakers was much lower), I'll never forget one phrase uttered by a brain surgeon who wanted to practice his English with me. He had either memorized set phrases from an old textbook or was translating from Ukrainian when he nonchalantly commented, "The weather is rather mood stabilising today, isn't it?" I encourage you to meet people, chat with them, and have fun with the cultural differences.

If you are looking to primarily meet other English speakers, in Kyiv there are a lot of expats from North America and Western Europe, and you can easily find expat groups through the Kyiv Post newspaper or groups advertised on the Internet. There are many events organized throughout the year, which are primarily attended by expats.

As mentioned, smiling in a North American way in Ukraine is not synonymous with "being friendly". Once you get to know them, most Ukrainians are very nice, joyful and touchingly sincere, Government employees, however, and a minority of "homo Sovieticus" type individuals, are another story. Those working at train stations, the Zhek utilities office, the post office, or the tax authority, for example, may be less polite. It can also be very frustrating when they seem to deliberately give you the least amount of information possible. For example, if you go to register for temporary residency at your local Zhek, and you ask the lady at the counter what the hours of operation are for her colleague across the hall who is in charge of utilities bills, her reply might be "Go ask her yourself",

"I don't know", or she might not acknowledge your question at all (since it's not in her job description to be aware of that).

The same is true with phone calls; don't be surprised and please don't take it personally if a public employee hangs up on you because they don't know the answer to your questions. I chalk this rude communication down to being a habit from Communist times when state employees were only required to provide bare minimum services; and to the fact that the pay is so low that these people don't feel like they are earning enough to go out of their way and be nice. My advice is to have a representative or helper in Ukraine who can sort through any local bureaucratic issues for you.

A completely contrary experience happened when I visited my dad's relatives in a village outside of Lviv for the first time in 1998. They were so hospitable and eager to share with us and show us how they lived, and they were bursting with excitement at having us visit their home. As is common in Ukrainian villages, when guests arrive they are invited to the table and are offered an alcoholic drink (often a shot of vodka) and food. In our case it was some little canapés, some with cheese, others topped with canned fish. They kept encouraging us to eat more, and my parents and I thought this was lunch, so we ate our fill. We were very surprised when the open-faced sandwiches were followed by soup, then homemade *varenyky* and cabbage rolls, which we barely had room for. Not to mention not having room for the selection of homemade cakes for dessert with coffee or tea. But at the table, Ukrainian hosts don't often take 'no' for an answer, as it is considered rude not to feed your guests, so they kept filling up our plates. Afterwards they offered to let us rest and let our food digest; then they showed us more of where they lived (and eagerly insisted I try their newly built homemade outdoor shower), before showing us more of their village.

In short, once there is a chance to get to know someone closer, you will see the true nature of Ukrainians. I, for one, am fond of learning about other people's lives and have found that there are always many interesting conversations to be had in Ukraine, from politics to childrearing, to learning foreign languages, to European history and more. It has also been my experience that practically every woman I have gotten to know, from friends to nannies and even some women I only met briefly, has, in a private conversation from the start, opened up and shared her "story", quickly moving the friendship from the stage of not really knowing each other, to that of being able to relate on a deeper level. I have always appreciated being able to learn from the life experiences of others (including many stories about childhood or failed relationships) and share a very warm connection.

In terms of romantic relationships, Ukraine doesn't seem to follow the same dating rules or practices as in the West. If two people meet and are interested in each other, they will often quickly move to a long-lasting serious relationship, spending most of their free time together, usually within a larger group of friends. Where foreigners are concerned, though, I have witnessed cultural clashes and confusion, and also manipulative behaviour by some unscrupulous women. There is still a trend towards marrying young in Ukraine and starting a family soon after. But Ukrainians, being often passionate types, also seem to tend to succumb to their emotions in perhaps a similar way as the French, and extra-marital affairs are relatively common (maybe in some cases due to young marriages), and according to recent statistics, over half of all marriages end in divorce. (UNDP, 2014)

Some other social norms to be aware of…

Keep in mind that looking at strangers is acceptable, and incidentally is widely practiced in Kyiv on the metro. When my Ukrainian cousin visited Germany for the first time she noticed that strangers in the street would avoid looking at each other or making eye contact, and to her this felt very "cold".

Living in Ukraine and other countries has helped me re-evaluate what is acceptable/not acceptable, rude/polite, or "common "courtesy and realise that it's very culturally based. I now find it quite funny to recall the times I met up with relatives after not having seen them a few years and one of their first comments was "You've lost weight, you look great!". In English speaking cultures, people are careful to be polite and avoid any "awkward" moments, whereas in Ukraine this doesn't seem to be something people pay much attention to, preferring to "call a spade a spade". It might be a challenge to not take offence at such a comment, but please keep in mind that it is not usually meant to be rude or mean and often Ukrainians feel they are being helpful by pointing out something. Note that Ukrainians also don't seem to have a very thick barrier or personal space.

When making plans with Ukrainians, it has been my experience that they don't always want to be pinned down to committing to a time and place, and sometimes prefer to first see how their day is working out before committing. Mobile phones allow them to call and alter plans if necessary, even changing plans at the last minute. If this happens, don't take it personally. When making future plans, a common reply might be "якщо Бог дасть" /jaksho Boh dast, meaning, "God willing, it will happen". This is similar to the Muslim phrase "inshallah").

Which brings us again to the topic of religion. As mentioned, Ukrainians are quite strong believers in God and it is very normal and acceptable to bring up your faith privately or publicly, as it is for the most part, a shared belief with most Ukrainians being Christian (either Orthodox or Greek Catholic). The term Слава Богу /Slava Bohu ("Glory be to God") is used very frequently to mean "Thank God!").

Something to be aware of that I do sometimes find problematic in Ukraine is the level of honesty. I was once in a university class consisting of both Ukrainians and expats and the topic of "common values" came up. The two most hotly debated values were punctuality, and honesty, with most Ukrainians participants strongly arguing that it was okay to tell a few white lies as long as no one got hurt. Coming back to Ukraine after being away for a couple of years, it does seem like I hear white lies on a daily basis, usually related to daily events, why someone is unable to show up for a commitment or some other excuse. What doesn't help is the fact that speech can be very vague in Ukrainian and prodding is not really acceptable. The issue of honesty is perhaps one of the reasons that bribery and corruption are still major problems in Ukraine.

This can be a real issue if you need to be able to trust someone (like a babysitter), and you don't feel you can. I think the best way to deal with this is to be aware of it, and be honest with the person you are dealing with, clearly communicating that honesty is important and if you can't trust them then the work relationship/ whatever might have to come to an end. Finding someone you trust is definitely possible, it just might not happen on the first try.

If you spend enough time in Ukraine, you might also get a feeling for the sad part of the culture, which I believe to be a collective psyche of repeated historical traumas. Scientists who studied descendants of Holocaust survivors have recently concluded that emotional trauma can be genetically passed on to future generations (Thomson, 2015). So it's no wonder that the whole Ukrainian nation can get emotional when being reminded of the horrors their countrymen have been through in the struggle for self preservation and independence of their nation, or that people sometimes appear to have a lack of hope that things will get better in the future, and take to complaining. Ukrainians might appear to have a mentality of inferiority, a "martyr syndrome", or that of needing to constantly be suffering. This is understandable if you take into consideration all the horrors experienced throughout Ukraine's history, including the *Holodomor* famine genocide, Stalinist purges, and historical persecution of those choosing to speak the Ukrainian language.

FINAL THOUGHTS

Now that you are armed with some valuable travel and cultural knowledge on how to make the most of your trip to Ukraine, be it a short or long stay, you are ready for the next step: setting the date.

If you are interested in spending time in Ukraine, and chances are you are if you picked up this book, I urge you to act quickly with your plans. Not only is now a great time to travel to Ukraine due to the favourable currency situation, but as mentioned, you have more of a chance of experiencing an "authentic Ukraine" the sooner you go. Please don't keep your plans a distant dream. Take the plunge and discover Ukraine today.

Each person's experience in Ukraine will be unique but I am confident and hopeful that you will have an amazing experience and you will fall in love with some of the many charms Ukraine has to offer. Safe and happy travels! Щасливої дороги! Shchaslyvoyi dorohy!

VISA REGULATIONS

Currently nationals from most countries are allowed to stay in Ukraine for 90 days without a visa. Before you go, though, make sure to check online or with your embassy the particular visa regulations for citizens of your country. You can find your country on this link to see if you are one of the countries that allows 90 day stays without a visa. *http://mfa.gov.ua/en/consular-affairs/entering-ukraine/visa-requirements-for-foreigners*

http://www.visitkievukraine.com/essential/immigration/

Temporary residency

Most of the foreigners working in Ukraine have temporary residency permits. According to the law firm "Lion's mark", a temporary permit may be issued based on:

"job placement in Ukraine;

- reunification with the family, where one spouse is a citizen of Ukraine;

- reunification with the family, where one of its members (spouse, children) has a temporary residence permit in Ukraine;

- implementation of international technical assistance (which is duly registered);

- work in a religious organization (preaching, performing religious rituals or other canonical activities);

- work in offices and representations of foreign organizations, companies or banks;

- cultural, educational, scientific work and volunteering;

- work as a correspondent or representative of a foreign mass media; , or education."

If you come to Ukraine and decide you would like to stay more than 90 days, you can look for paid or volunteer work. If you find a position, the organization will likely help you with the documentation.

There are law firms that can offer assistance in obtaining residency permits for a fee. You can see the options and prices of one law firm on the following website: *http://lionsmark.com.ua/en/C/C2E.html*

Permanent residency

It is possible to remain a temporary resident for the whole time you are living in Ukraine. If you become a permanent resident, you can stay as long as you want without being tied to a particular job. This is possible if you have Ukrainian heritage or are married to a Ukrainian.

Lion's Mark provides information on permanent residency, along with their services and prices, on their website. The info below is taken from their site:

The first group - the persons within the immigration quota. The list of categories under the quota is stated in Article 4 of the Act.

They are:

1. Artists and scientists necessary for the country;

2. Highly qualified specialists needed in Ukraine;

3. Persons who invested in the economy of Ukraine $ 100 000 and more;

4. Full (siblings) brother, sister, grandfather, grandmother, grandson, granddaughter of the citizen of Ukraine;

5. Persons who have previously been Ukrainian citizens;

6. Parents, spouse and minor children of immigrants (the person who obtained permanent residence);

7. Refugees and persons who received asylum (after 3 years of residence);

8. Victims of trafficking (after 3 years of establishing the status).

The second group - the persons who may become immigrants in addition to the quota.

They are:

1. One spouse if the other spouse, with whom he was married for over two years, is a citizen of Ukraine;

2. Children and parents of citizens of Ukraine;

3. Persons who are eligible for citizenship of Ukraine by territorial origin;

4. Persons who are guardians or trustees of citizens of Ukraine, or who are in ward or under the tutelage of citizens of Ukraine;

5. Persons whose immigration is of state interest for Ukraine;

6. Ukrainians abroad, foreign spouses of Ukrainians, their children, in case of common entry and residence on the territory of Ukraine.

###

Thank you for reading my book. If you enjoyed it, would you please take a moment to leave me a review at your favourite online book retailer?

ABOUT THE AUTHOR

Maria Kachmar is a Ukrainian-Canadian educator and linguist. She has lived and worked in Ukraine, Germany, Poland, France, Austria and Qatar and appreciates the insights that can be gained from living internationally. Some of her interests include child development, child multilingualism, Ukrainian arts, yoga, healthy cooking and environmentalism. She enjoys spending time outdoors with her family.

Like my book on Facebook:
https://www.facebook.com/UkraineEuropesBestKeptSecret/

Other Books by Maria Kachmar
Semestr u Lvovi, pryhody i vrazhennia kanadskoi studentky, 2001

A Semester in Lviv, 2016 (English language translation the above book)

BIBLIOGRAPHY

Beauplan, Guillaume Le Vasseur, sieur de, (1861). Description de l'Vkranie depvis les confins dc la Moscovie jvsqu'avx limites de la Transylvanie. Paris: J. Techner., Internet Archive

Paszczak Tracz, Orysia. "THE THINGS WE DO...: The Koza at Christmas (01/09/05)." THE THINGS WE DO...: The Koza at Christmas (01/09/05). The Ukrainian Weekly, 29 Jan. 2009. Web. 14 Feb. 2016.

Thomson, Helen. "Study of Holocaust Survivors Finds Trauma Passed on to Children's Genes | Science | The Guardian." *The Guardian.* The Guardian, 21 Aug.2015. Web. 17 Feb. 2016.

Butkevych, Bohdan. "Marriage: Easy Come, Easy Go." *The Ukrainian Week.* N.p., 17 Dec. 2012. Web. 17 Feb. 2016.

UNDP. "Young Couples in Ukraine to Be Better Prepared for Married Life | UNDP in Ukraine." N.p., Apr. 2014. Web.

"Ukraine." *UNESCO.* N.p., n.d. Web. 17 Feb. 2016. <http://en.unesco.org/countries/ukraine>.

Popova, Y. (2012, February 9). Tracing the coffee house revolution to its Ukrainian roots. *BBC Travel.* Retrieved from http://www.bbc.com/travel/story/20120124-tracing-the-coffee-house-revolution-to-its-ukrainian-roots

Siundiukov, Ihor. "Guillaume De Beauplan and "the Land of the Cossacks" | The Day Newspaper." *Guillaume De Beauplan and "the Land of the Cossacks".* N.p., 12 Dec. 2016. Web. 17 Feb. 2016.

"Boim Chapel." *Wikipedia, the Free Encyclopedia.* Wikimedia Foundation, Inc, 2015. Web. 17 Feb. 2016.

"Vysokyi Zamok (High Castle) (Високий Замок): Lviv's Highest PointLviv Alive." *Lviv Alive.* N.p., 2012. Web. 17 Feb. 2016.

"Палац Потоцьких (Львів) — Вікіпедія." *Вікіпедія.* 2013. Web. 17 Feb. 2016.

"Палац Бандінеллі — Вікіпедія." *Вікіпедія.* 2013. Web. 18 Feb. 2016.

"Zoological Museum of Lviv National University Named After Ivan

логічний музей Львівського національного університету імені
..a. N.p., n.d. Web. 18 Feb. 2016.

.live | Museum | Brewing Museum (Музей Пивоваріння):
.rs to Ukraine's Oldest BreweryLviv Alive." *Lviv Alive.* N.p., n.d.
..b. 28 Feb. 2016.

"Andrey Sheptytsky National Museum in Lviv - Culture - Cultural
Institutions - Things to Do."*Lviv.travel - Official City Guide.* Lviv City
Council, n.d. Web. 28 Feb. 2016.

"Anna of Kyiv, Queen of France." *Welcome to Ukraine.* N.p., n.d. Web.
18 Feb. 2016.

"Anna Yaroslavna." *Home, Encyclopedia of Ukraine.* N.p., 2010. Web.
28 Feb. 2016.

"Golden Gate." *Home, Encyclopedia of Ukraine.* 2001. Web.
18 Feb. 2016.

Subtelny, Orest. "Bendery, Constitution of." *Home, Encyclopedia of
Ukraine.* N.p., 1984. Web. 28 Feb. 2016.

"Saint Sophia's Cathedral, Kiev." *Wikipedia, the Free Encyclopedia.*
Wikimedia Foundation, Inc, 2016. Web. 27 Feb. 2016.

Pavlovsky, Vadym, and Arkadii Zhukovsky. "Saint Michael's Golden-
Domed Monastery."*Home, Encyclopedia of Ukraine.* N.p., 2004. Web.
28 Feb. 2016.

"Saint Andrew's Church." *Home, Encyclopedia of Ukraine.*
N.p., 1993. Web. 28 Feb. 2016.

"Святий апостол Андрій Первозванний | Андріївська

церква." *Андріївська церква в Києві УАПЦ.* N.p., n.d. Web. 28 Feb. 2016.

Pavlovsky, Vadym. "Kyivan Cave Monastery." *Home, Encyclopedia of
Ukraine.* N.p., 1989. Web. 28 Feb. 2016.

*Олешківські піски: T2210 - Стежками України! | stezhkamu.com. (n.d.).
Retrieved from http://stezhkamu.com/places/392_oleshkivski_pisky*

*Камяна Могила — Вікіпедія. (2016). Retrieved from
https://uk.wikipedia.org/wiki/Камяна_Могила*